# MARRIAGE, DIVORCE, REMARRIAGE

# SOCIAL TRENDS IN THE UNITED STATES

# Marriage, Divorce, Remarriage

## Revised and Enlarged Edition

» Andrew J. Cherlin

HARVARD UNIVERSITY PRESS
Cambridge, Massachusetts
London, England
1992

Library of Congress Cataloging-in-Publication Data

Cherlin, Andrew J., 1948–
    Marriage, divorce, remarriage / Andrew J. Cherlin.—Rev. and
enl. ed.
        p.  cm.—(Social trends in the United States)
        Includes bibliographical references and index.
        ISBN 0-674-55082-X
        1. Marriage—United States.  2. Divorce—United States.  3. Remarriage—United
States.  4. Family—United States.  5. Afro-American families.  I. Title.  II. Series.
HQ535.C415 1992
306.8'0973—dc20        91-47163

# Contents

# Preface

When I looked over *Marriage, Divorce, Remarriage* some six years after its publication in 1981, I concluded that some of the information was becoming dated. Statistics needed to be updated, new research findings needed to be cited, and some of the analysis and interpretation of the numbers needed to be revised. Four years and several intervening projects later, I finished work on this edition, which is somewhere between a major revision and a new book.

The title I gave the first edition was intended to convey the course of family life for an increasing number of Americans: a marriage, then a divorce, then a remarriage. But developments in the 1970s and 1980s suggest that family lives are more varied and can be even more complex. If there were a truth-in-labeling law for books, the title of this edition should be something long and unwieldy like *Cohabitation, Marriage, Divorce, More Cohabitation, and Probably Remarriage.* In this edition, I describe and interpret new research findings about the rise of cohabitation and its relationship to marriage. Later in the book, I discuss the weakening of marriage as an institution and its meaning for contemporary Americans.

Those who have read the 1981 edition will find the basic structure of the first three chapters familiar. Chapter 1 describes the demographic trends since World War II. It incorporates many updated new statistics, a more extensive discussion of cohabitation, and other new material. Chapter 2 discusses the explanations that have been advanced for these trends. It incorporates some new historical and sociological scholarship on family life during the last half of the twentieth century. This new research has caused me to revise my position on the causes of developments such as the baby boom and bust. In this chapter, I describe two kinds of explanations: cohort-based and period-based. Whereas the earlier edition gave more or less equal weight to both, I now lean more toward period-based explanations. Chapter 3, on the consequences of the trends, now incorporates information from the many new studies during the 1980s of the effects of divorce and remarriage on adults and children.

Chapter 4 of the 1981 edition examined racial differences in marriage patterns. During the 1980s, few issues received more attention from social scientists than the connections among race, poverty, and the family. This chapter has been entirely rewritten for this edition. It now ranges more broadly over the issues, and it presents and evaluates information from many recent studies. I have added a fifth and final chapter, in which I assess the state of the family and the implications of the massive changes during the last half of the twentieth century.

During the years in which I grappled with this ever-expanding revision, many people read and commented on the chapters or provided me with statistics. They include: Nan Astone, Larry Bumpass, Lindsay Chase-Lansdale, Renbao Chen, David Ellwood, M. D. R. Evans, Frank F. Furstenberg, Jr., Christopher Jencks, Karen Mason, Antonio McDaniel, Sara McLanahan, Philip Morgan, Samuel Preston, Ronald Rindfuss, Robert Schoen, James Sweet, Arland Thornton, and Susan Watkins. I thank them all; and I also thank Michael Aronson for his patience and support. Michele Trieb ably prepared the charts and graphs.

Parts of Chapter 5 appeared as "The Strange Career of the 'Harvard-Yale Study'" in *Public Opinion Quarterly,* copyright 1990 by the American Association for Public Opinion Research. Parts of Chapter 3 appeared as "Remarriage as an Incomplete Institution," in *American Journal of Sociology,* copyright 1978 by the University of Chicago Press. Both are reprinted by permission of the University of Chicago Press.

There still are gaps in this book. I think the most glaring is the lack of information on Hispanic families. The category "Hispanic" took on a political life of its own in the 1980s. The differences among Hispanic families, however, are nearly as great as the differences between Hispanic and non-Hispanic families. Only within the last few years has information become available on the subgroups in the Hispanic population, particularly Mexican Americans, Puerto Ricans, and Cuban Americans, although it is still thin. In addition, the book does not cover the family lives of gay people, a topic of growing interest. Here again, good information is scarce. More studies on these subjects should appear during this decade. If I am fortunate enough to publish a third edition ten years from now, I will include more information about the family lives of Hispanics and gays.

November 1991

# Marriage, Divorce, Remarriage

# Introduction

Consider the following hypothetical life history. When Bill was ten, his parents separated and divorced. He lived with his mother and saw his father every Saturday. Four years later, his mother remarried, and Bill added a stepfather to his family. At eighteen, Bill left home to attend college, and after graduation he and his girlfriend moved in together. A year and a half later they married, and soon afterward they had a child. After several years, however, the marriage began to turn sour. Bill and his wife eventually divorced, with Bill's wife retaining custody of the child. Three years later Bill married a woman who had a child from a previous marriage, and together they had another child. Bill's second marriage lasted thirty-five years, until his death.

By the time he entered middle age, Bill had lived in six family or family-like settings: first in his parents' household, then in a single-parent family headed by his mother, then in a family formed by his mother's remarriage, then in a cohabiting relationship with his girlfriend, then in his first marriage, and finally in his second marriage. He had accumulated a large number of kin and quasi-kin: his mother, father, stepfather, first wife, second wife, two children, and his stepchild, not to mention more distant kin such as grandparents, stepgrandparents, and two sets of in-laws. At one time or another he had had dealings with people to whom he was related only by the ties of broken marriages, such as his father's second wife, his first wife's second husband, and his second wife's first husband.

Most young people today won't pass through all of the events in this example, but if the levels of marriage, divorce, remarriage, and cohabitation don't decrease in the near future, many will. And many more will have family histories only slightly less complicated. In the 1950s someone with a family history this complex would have been rare; in the 1990s it is no longer unusual. The contrast between the 1990s and the 1950s might lead us to ask: Why are the common patterns of marrying and divorcing so different from what they were just a few decades ago? And what are the consequences of these changes for the lives of adults and children and for our society as a whole?

In the late 1940s and the 1950s young adults tended to marry earlier than they had at anytime during the century, the birth rate rose to a twentieth-century high, and the divorce rate remained unusually steady. But in the 1960s and 1970s the average age at marriage rose, the birth rate dropped to an all-time low, and the divorce rate more than doubled. In the 1980s and early 1990s, marriage rates at first fell further and then stabilized, and birth and divorce rates changed more slowly. Since about 1980, then, we have had an interval of less rapid change in marriage and divorce—a period in which we can pause to take stock of the changes that have occurred in recent decades, to investigate the causes of these changes, and to examine their likely consequences.

During the early 1970s, as wave after wave of statistics about the changes in family life washed into our consciousness through news reports and scholarly accounts, a number of commentators predicted that the family as we know it would not survive much longer. These forebodings are nothing new: for at least a century American observers have warned of the consequences of rising incidence of divorce, falling birth rates, and other changes in family life. "The family, in its old sense," wrote a contributor to the *Boston Quarterly Review* of October 1859, "is disappearing from our land, and not only our free institutions are threatened but the very existence of our society is endangered."[1] Whenever the pace of change quickens—particularly when the divorce rate is increasing rapidly—these sentiments reappear. When concern about divorce grew in the 1970s, however, some scholars countered with evidence that the changes had been exaggerated and that in any case the family was a flexible institution that was unlikely to fade away.[2] By the end of the 1970s, when the pace of change had slowed again, the more sanguine view had prevailed.

Nevertheless, all the commentators agreed that the postwar changes in family patterns had significantly altered the lives of many Americans. Although the family undoubtedly has a future, its present form differs from its past form in important respects, at least in part because of the recent changes in patterns of cohabiting, marrying, divorcing, and remarrying. A smaller proportion of families today than in the 1950s resemble the two-biological-parents-with-children family which has been the norm in the United States. Instead, a greater proportion consist of single parents and their children or families formed by remarriage after divorce. Because of the sharp rise in divorce, the common assumption that a family occupies one household is increasingly incorrect. Although separation and divorce break the bonds between father and mother, the bonds between children and parents tend to remain intact. Consequently, an increasing number of families extend across two or three or more households, linked by the continuing ties between parents and children who live apart. Under these circumstances kinship ties are more complex and far-reaching than in families formed by first marriages. And even the definition of a family can become problematic—a child whose mother and father have divorced and remarried may define the members of his family differently than either parent does.

The roller-coaster pattern of rapid change in marriage and divorce in the period from the end of World War II to the late 1970s may itself have strained the capacity of the family to adapt, much as rapid change would strain the adaptive capacity of any social institution. The rapid pace also may have strained our capacity to make sense out of what has been going on. Just as we arrived at an understanding of the changes in family life, the trends shifted again. It may be useful, consequently, to look back over family change during the entire postwar period from the vantage point of the early 1990s.

Family change is a broad topic, and any coherent report must be selective in its coverage. Because my focus is on the formation and dissolution of marriage and its causes and consequences, I do not have much to say about many other significant trends in husband-wife or parent-child relationships. For example, during the postwar period the proportion of two-parent families in which both husband and wife were employed increased sharply. These families faced new and challenging problems in integrating their work lives with satisfying family lives. Regrettably, a detailed discussion of these problems would take us too far afield.

Nor is this a report on trends in childbearing, an important topic that is complex enough to deserve a book of its own. Yet because there are obviously close connections between trends in marriage and divorce and trends in childbearing, I do examine some aspects of childbearing. As a study of overall trends in American society in the last several decades, this book does not include much discussion of the differences among ethnic, religious, and regional groups. There is evidence that many intergroup differences have declined in the postwar period. For instance, as I note below, Catholics appear to have become more similar to Protestants in their childbearing patterns and in their propensity to divorce. In addition, we lack adequate data on many group differences. The statements I make in the first three chapters, then, apply to Americans in general, although I try to alert the reader when there are sharp deviations among particular groups. Yet strong racial differences exist in many aspects of family life, including marriage and divorce, and some of these differences have become more pronounced during the postwar period. For this reason, in Chapter 4 I discuss the differences between the typical patterns of marriage among blacks and whites.

My focus also means that I do not examine many of the so-called alternative life styles to marriage: communal living, gay couples, lifelong singlehood, and so forth. Although these ways of living are interesting in their own right, on a societal level the number of people involved in them is small compared to the number of ever-married persons—although growing in the cases of lifelong singlehood and possibly gay couples. I do, however, discuss the great increase in cohabitation since about 1970. I also examine the growth of single-parent families—much of which can be traced to the increase in separation and divorce—and the consequences of living in these families as a parent or as a child.

My first task is to take a long, hard look at the demographic data on trends in marriage, divorce, and remarriage, as well as the trends in such closely allied topics as cohabitation, single-parent families, and childbearing. Only by determining rigorously what did and did not happen to families in the postwar period is it possible to amass the factual base needed to probe the causes and consequences of the trends. The indicators I examine in Chapter 1 should help us decide where to look for explanations of the trends and point to the important consequences. Moreover, a careful look at the record should disabuse us of any misleading common notions about the trends. For example, there is evidence to contradict the conventional wisdom that the family patterns of the 1970s and 1980s were more unusual, in a historical sense, than the family patterns of the 1950s. Chapter 2 examines promising explanations, and Chapter 3 explores the consequences of the trends for husbands and wives and for parents and children. Chapter 4 looks at the differences between the family patterns of black and white Americans and assesses the implications of these differences for the movement of families into and out of poverty. Finally, in Chapter 5, I stand back and examine the meaning of all of these changes for the institution of marriage.

# 1

# Demographic Trends

We often think of social change in terms of the differences between one generation and the next—between our parents' lives and our own lives or between our own lives and our children's lives. When we look at the trends in marriage, divorce, and remarriage in the United States since World War II, the experiences of two successive generations stand in sharp contrast: the men and women who married and had children in the late 1940s and 1950s, and their sons and daughters, who entered adulthood in the late 1960s and 1970s. Most of the members of the older generation were born in the 1920s and the 1930s, and they grew up during the Great Depression and World War II. This group is relatively small because fewer babies were born during the late 1920s and the hard times of the 1930s. But when they reached adulthood, this generation had a relatively large number of children. About five out of six of the women whose peak childbearing years occurred in the 1950s gave birth to at least two children, and those births were bunched at an earlier time in their lives.[1] The result was a great increase in births between the end of World War II and the early 1960s, an increase which we now call the postwar baby boom. In 1957, at the peak of the boom, 4.3 million babies were born in the United States, compared to 2.4 million in 1937. Thus the small generation of parents in the 1950s gave birth to a much larger generation—the baby boomers.[2]

In the 1950s, when the members of the older generation were in their twenties and thirties, the country's marriage rate was high and rising, and its divorce rate was relatively low and stable. But as the younger generation matured, all that changed. The divorce rate began to rise in the early 1960s and doubled between 1966 and 1976. As more and more of the baby boomers put off marrying, the marriage rate fell, and the birth rate plummeted to an all-time low.

Now, as we approach the twenty-first century, a third generation—

the children of the baby boomers—are beginning to reach adulthood. It is too soon to know for sure what their family lives will be like, but the broad outlines seem clear. During the 1980s the divorce rate declined slightly but remained high enough that about half of all marriages, at current rates, would end in divorce. And although the birth rate rebounded from its low point in 1972, it remained at a modest average of two births per woman. Young adults continued to postpone marrying, and cohabitation became so common that a majority of the third generation probably will live with a partner before marriage.

In this chapter I compare the experiences of the two older generations as they have married, had children, divorced, and remarried; and I discuss the likely experiences of the third generation. But we must be careful not to assume that just because the oldest generation came first, their family patterns were more typical of twentieth-century American family life. Put another way, we shouldn't assume that all the changes since the 1950s were deviations from the usual way of family life in the United States. In fact, I argue that the 1950s were the more unusual time, that the timing of marriage in the 1970s and 1980s was closer to the typical twentieth-century pattern than was the case in the 1950s. In addition, the rate of childbearing in the 1950s was unusually high by twentieth-century standards. In some ways the 1970s and 1980s were more consistent with long-term trends in family life than were the 1950s.

Nevertheless, the 1970s and 1980s were distinctive. Whereas fewer marriages begun in the 1950s ended in divorce than the historical trend would predict, more marriages begun in the 1970s ended in divorce than would have been predicted. Moreover, during the 1970s and 1980s, living with a partner outside of marriage became accepted, even commonplace. And by the end of the 1980s, the average age at marriage for women was at a twentieth-century high.

In order to back up statements such as these, the mass of statistical information on family life must be shaped into a coherent picture of the lifetime experiences of men and women. That requires a clear definition of two key terms: "cohort" and "generation." By a cohort, I mean a group of people who were born during the same time period. The period can be one year or several years, depending on the kinds of topics being investigated. By a generation, I mean a group of people who are the ascendent or descendent kin of another group: grandparents, parents, children, grandchildren, and so on.

A generation usually comprises several successive cohorts; just how many depends on how narrowly we define the time period for each cohort. Take, for example, the men and women who had children during the late 1940s and the 1950s. It is sometimes useful to think of these people as a generation because they are the parents of the children of the baby boom. Most of these parents were born in the 1920s and 1930s, although a small minority were born earlier and a handful were born later. We could conceivably consider everyone born between 1920 and 1939 as members of one cohort. Yet the experiences of a person born in 1920 (who was nine when the depression began) were probably quite different from the experiences of someone born in 1936 (who was nine when World War II ended). In studying the parental generation of the 1950s, then, it may be more enlightening to separate them into at least two cohorts—those born in the 1920s and those born in the 1930s—and investigate their differing lifetime experiences. Demographers use the term "cohort analysis" to refer to this strategy of dividing a generation into its constituent cohorts and tracing the lifetime experiences of each.

## Marriage and Cohabitation

Although it is hard to imagine now, getting married within weeks of graduation was a symbol of success for many college-educated women in the 1950s and early 1960s. "Ring by spring or your money back" was a popular saying among coeds (the now antiquated term for female undergraduates) in a generation in which half of all women married before age 21. Anyone who knows young adults today realizes that more and more of them are postponing marriage until their mid- or late twenties or even their thirties. Since 1970, there also has been a spectacular increase in the number of adults who have moved in with someone of the opposite sex without marrying first. Some observers have expressed concern that the later age at marriage and the increase in cohabitation (or "living together") might indicate a weakening of our system of marriage and family life. Others are more sanguine but accept that these changing patterns of coupling have greatly altered American family life.

Throughout the twentieth century, about nine out of ten Americans eventually married, although in some eras people tended to marry earlier than in others. Those who married earliest were the men and women who were born during the depression and the war years. Figure 1-1 graphs the percentage of women and men twenty to twenty-four years old who had never married from 1890—the earliest year for which we have information—to 1990. This is the age range in which the greatest swings in marriage timing have occurred. We can see from this graph that the percentages changed very little between 1890 and 1940.

*Figure 1-1.* Percentage never married for men and women aged 20 to 24, 1890 to 1990. Sources: for 1890–1960, U.S. Bureau of the Census, *Historical Statistics of the United States, Colonial Times to 1970,* pp. 20–21; for 1970 to 1989, *Current Population Reports,* Series P-20, no. 445, "Marital Status and Living Arrangements: March 1989," table B; for 1990, *Current Population Reports,* Series P-20, no. 450, "Marital Status and Living Arrangements: March 1990," table B.

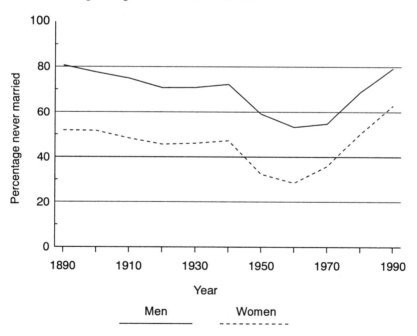

But after 1940, when those who were born in the 1920s entered adulthood, the percentage never married decreased sharply. It stayed low during the years when people born during the depression and the war reached their early twenties. Then in the 1970s, as the men and women born during the baby boom reached their early twenties, the percentage never married turned upward. In the 1980s, the upward trend continued. The percentage never married has now returned to its earlier, higher levels for men and has even exceeded the earlier levels for women.

Consequently, although some commentators have argued that the trend toward later marriage in the 1970s and 1980s represented a deviation from traditional patterns of family formation, the historical record is more complex. The timing of marriage among the male baby boomers, who tended to marry in the 1970s and 1980s, and their sons, who are starting to marry now, is in line with the pattern observed in the 1890 to 1940 period. It is the fathers of the baby boomers, the men born between the early 1920s and World War II, whose behavior is problematic. To say that in the 1970s and 1980s men were "postponing" marriage is justifiable only if the unusual decade of the 1950s is chosen as the frame of reference. Among women, the mothers of the baby boomers married at earlier ages than any other generation in the twentieth century. In the 1970s, their daughters married at older, more typical ages. But the average age at marriage kept increasing in the 1980s and now is older than at any time in this century. In Chapter 2, I will discuss why the timing of marriage has fluctuated so sharply since mid-century.[3]

These changes do not necessarily imply that large numbers of the young adults of the 1980s will remain unmarried throughout their lives. More than 90 percent of the women in every birth cohort on record (records extend back to the mid-1800s) have eventually married.[4] The adults who came of age after World War II have the highest lifetime percentage married—96.4 percent for females and 94.1 percent for males who were at their most marriageable ages in the 1950s—and it is highly unlikely that their children and grandchildren will reach this level.[5] In fact, recent estimates suggest that the lifetime percentage married among women born during the baby boom may fall below the historical minimum of 90 percent by a percentage point or two.[6] Still, the higher proportion of single young adults in the 1980s suggests mainly that they are marrying later, not forgoing marriage. This is so at least for whites; for blacks there has been a far deeper decline in marriage. In Chapter 4, I will compare marriage patterns among blacks and whites.

Although young adults are postponing marriage, they aren't postponing living with a partner nearly as much. Since 1970 there has been a great increase in cohabitation—that is, in couples not married to each other who live in the same household. Figure 1-2 displays the trend, based on life histories of persons in the 1987–88 National Survey of Families and Households (NSFH). It shows the percentage of people in several birth cohorts, beginning about 1930, who cohabited by age 25, according to education. For example, the darkest bar tracks the percentage of persons without a high school degree who cohabited in the various cohorts. The reader can see that cohabitation was rare among people born about 1930 (who came of age in the 1950s), and was largely confined to those without a college education. Although little is known about these partnerships, it is likely that many were long-term, consensual unions among the poor and near-poor. Evidence from many societies suggests that couples with low incomes and unstable jobs are less likely to marry. With few assets to divide and little property to pass on, there is less reason for them to seek the recognition and protection of marriage laws.[7]

But starting with people born about 1940, cohabitation began to increase among young adults regardless of their level of education. Among those born about 1950, who entered adulthood after 1970, the rise became sharper. When cohabitation became noticeable among middle-class young adults in the 1970s, conventional wisdom was that recent college graduates, rejecting the values of their parents, had started the trend. But Figure 1-2 shows that college graduates were not the trendsetters; at all times over the past several decades, persons with less education were more likely to cohabit. To be sure, there was a sharp rise in cohabitation among college graduates in the 1970s, so the claim that they were radically changing their behavior was correct. But so was everyone else. It seems likely that college graduates attracted the atten-

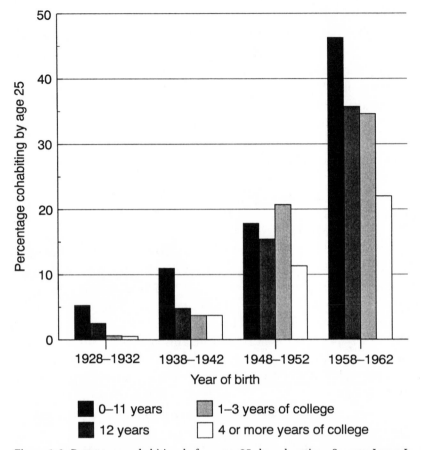

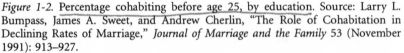

*Figure 1-2.* Percentage cohabiting before age 25, by education. Source: Larry L. Bumpass, James A. Sweet, and Andrew Cherlin, "The Role of Cohabitation in Declining Rates of Marriage," *Journal of Marriage and the Family* 53 (November 1991): 913–927.

tion of the media and academics because they were the most visible component of a widespread phenomenon. College graduates were not the innovators in cohabitation but rather the imitators.

Cohabitation is now so prevalent that a majority of the third postwar generation—the offspring of the baby boom children—likely will live with a partner before marrying. According to the NSFH, just 11 percent of persons who married between 1965 and 1974 cohabited with someone beforehand, compared to 32 percent of those who married between 1975 and 1979, and 44 percent of those who married between 1980 and 1984.[8] The percentage was probably even higher for persons marrying in the late 1980s.[9] Moreover, cohabitation is even more widespread among the previously married than among the never-married. Sixty percent of persons in the NSFH who married for a second time in the 1980s had lived with someone beforehand.[10] It already is the case, then, that a large majority of remarriages are preceded by a period of cohabitation.

Because of the increase in cohabitation, young adults are nearly as likely to be sharing a household with a partner as they were in 1970, despite marrying much later. Let us define a *union* as a couple who are either cohabiting or married. Figure 1-3 shows the changes between 1970 and 1985 in the percentage of 25-year-olds who had ever been in

*Figure 1-3.* Percentage ever-married and ever in a union by age 25, 1970 and 1985. Source: Bumpass, Sweet, and Cherlin, "The Role of Cohabitation in Declining Rates of Marriage."

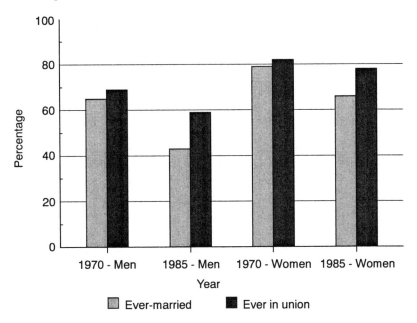

a union. In 1970, nearly everyone who had been in a union had been married; very few had just lived with someone. Between 1970 and 1985, as the lighter bars show, the percentage of men and women who had ever married declined sharply. But the numbers who had only cohabited increased nearly as sharply. As a result, the proportion who had ever been in a union of either kind (the darker bars) declined only modestly. In fact, during these fifteen years the rise in cohabitation compensated for 59 percent of the decline in marriage for men and 76 percent of the decline in marriage for women. At the end of the period, young adults were nearly as likely to be in a union, but a much smaller proportion of these unions were legal marriages.[11]

This is not to say that cohabitation and marriage mean the same thing to individuals but rather that the differences are sometimes overstated. When the rise in cohabitation first attracted attention in the early 1970s, some researchers believed it to be a radical departure from traditional patterns of family formation. "The living together relationship," wrote two scholars in 1973, "may come to represent a universal substitute for marriage for adults of all ages."[12] But that hasn't happened, at least not in the United States. Studies have shown that cohabiting couples tend to live together for a relatively short time before either breaking up or marrying. About half of all cohabiting relationships result in either marriage or a break-up within one-and-one-half years, and 90 percent do so within five years.[13] When cohabiting relationships end, about 60 percent result in marriage and 40 percent in a break-up.[14]

The evidence suggests, then, that for a majority of young adults cohabitation is not a lifelong alternative to marriage but rather a stage of intimacy that precedes (or sometimes follows) marriage. These young adults appear to be cohabiting as a way of finding a compatible partner, whom they often marry. When given a list of reasons why persons might want to live together, cohabitors under age 35 in the NSFH most often selected "couples can be sure they are compatible before marriage." Moreover, 47 percent of never-married cohabitors said that they had definite plans to marry their partner, and 27 percent said that they thought they would marry their partner.[15] It may be, then, that the increase in cohabitation will have little effect on the lifetime chances that a young adult will ever marry.

Still, not all who cohabit expect, or even desire, marriage. For some, cohabitation is a convenient way to obtain intimacy without making a long-term commitment.[16] Cohabiting adults in the NSFH were asked a series of questions about whether aspects of their lives such as economic security or overall happiness might be better, the same, or worse if they were to marry. By far the most common response was "the same." For example, 71 percent of men and 72 percent of women said that their relationship with their parents would remain the same, whereas only 22 and 24 percent, respectively, said it would be better.[17] Cohabiting adults seem to feel little pressure to marry. Moreover, one out of six of the never-married couples in the NSFH had borne a child since they began to live together.

Some writers argued in the 1970s that cohabitation would enhance personal growth, lead to a better choice of marriage partners, and lower the divorce rate.[18] To be sure, cohabitation often is a trial relationship, a way for men and women to develop and test feelings of intimacy and to assess their mutual compatibility. It is reasonable to expect that some incompatible couples who might have married and then divorced had they been born a decade or two earlier will now cohabit and then separate without ever marrying. These *de facto* divorces will never show up in the divorce rate. To the extent, then, that cohabitation allows adults to refine their criteria for choosing spouses and to dissolve unsuccessful relationships, it might be expected to lower the amount of divorce.

Yet it now appears that marriages that follow cohabitation have a higher rate of dissolution than do marriages that begin without cohabitation. In the NSFH, marriages begun after cohabitation were one-third more likely to break up during the first ten years; and similar results have been reported in other studies.[19] Cohabitation carries with it the ethic that a relationship should be ended if either partner is dissatisfied; this, after all, is part of the reason why people live together rather than marrying. Most people who choose to cohabit either subscribe to this individualistic ethic beforehand or soon learn to do so, and they bring this ethic to their marriages. On the other hand, unmarried adults who do not cohabit probably have a more traditional view of the sanctity of the marriage bond, and they bring this traditional attitude to their marriages. Consequently, the spread of cohabitation involves the spread of an individualistic outlook on intimate relations, an outlook that makes people more likely to dissolve a union—whether marital or not—if they find it personally unfulfilling.

The phenomenon of cohabitation is so new in the United States that it is hard to know how it will develop in the years ahead. Western Europe offers two models, the Swedish and French cases. In both countries long-term cohabitation is more common, but in Sweden the changes have gone further. Living together before marriage is virtually universal in Sweden: by the late 1970s, 96 percent of women who married had cohabited first.[20] And only 20 percent of the cohabiting couples married within three years of starting to live together, compared to 49 percent of American cohabiting couples.[21] Having a first child out of wedlock—but in a cohabiting relationship—is the norm in Sweden, where by the end of the 1980s about half of all births occurred to cohabiting women.[22] Clearly, cohabitation is much more of a substitute for marriage in Sweden than in the United States. During the 1970s and 1980s, marriage rates plunged in Sweden as many young couples seemed to abandon marriage altogether. By 1980, 15 percent of all Swedish households consisted of a cohabiting couple, compared to 2 percent in the United States.[23]

Midway between the United States and Sweden is the case of France, where living together is more common than in the United States—6 percent of all households consisted of a cohabiting couple in 1982—but far from universal.[24] Cohabiting relationships last longer, on average, in France: 30 percent last at least five years as compared to 10 percent in the United States. In a 1985 French national survey, half of all cohabiting adults responded that they "did not think about marriage" and only 26 percent said that they wanted to "marry quickly."[25] When shown a list of advantages of marriage, only "the good of children" was cited by more than half as a decisive reason for them to marry. And those who wanted children were twice as likely to say that they wished to marry. The authors of the study concluded that for most persons, cohabitation is a "neutral" phase of life, one in which the partners want to leave their options open, and in which neither person is thinking much about marrying or having children in the near future.

Does either of these countries provide a guide to what might be happening in the United States? Americans tend to watch Sweden for hints about the future, as if any new social trend in Scandinavia automatically hits California a few years later and then seeps slowly eastward. But the Scandinavian countries have a long tradition of cohabitation; in past centuries, rural couples often lived together before marriage, and many children were born out of wedlock.[26] Rural Swedes often felt that the decision to marry was a private matter; Americans have always believed that marriage should be publicly approved by church and state. This difference, I think, makes it unlikely that cohabitation and out-of-wedlock births ever will be as widespread here as in Sweden.

It is possible, although by no means certain, that cohabitation could evolve toward the French model (which is itself still evolving). In that case, cohabiting unions would become even more common than they are today, and they would last somewhat longer, on average. More important, the norms in favor of marriage would erode further—leaving little reason to marry except for the good of the children. But even that reason would lose some of its force as out-of-wedlock births to cohabiting couples became more acceptable and as legal protection was extended to the children. Most people still would marry eventually, but a sizeable minority would not. Of course, it's also possible that American society won't move further in this direction.

So far, at least, neither the increase in cohabitation nor the later age at marriage has produced major changes in patterns of marriage, divorce, and remarriage. To be sure, these trends have altered the life course of young adults; in two decades cohabitation has added an unprecedented new stage of intimacy. But as of now, this new stage of intimacy leads rapidly, for most people, to the rejection of unsatisfactory partners and to the eventual choice of one partner as worthy of a long-term public commitment. Most Americans continue to make this commitment in the form of marriage, although they may take a few years longer to do so than did the generation reaching adulthood in the 1950s.

## Childbearing

Trends in childbearing also demonstrate the sharp differences between the parental generation of the 1950s and their children's generation. Most people are familiar with the broad outlines of the postwar trend in childbearing, or fertility, to use the demographer's term for childbearing: the annual birth rate spurted upward just after the war and, after a brief respite, increased sharply during the 1950s. It then fell just as sharply in the 1960s and 1970s and remained low in the 1980s. We now know that during the 1950s women were having their first child earlier in their lives, and subsequent children were born closer together; after 1960 women had their first child at a later age and spaced subsequent children farther apart.[27] These trends in the timing of fertility— the accelerated pace of the 1950s and the postponement of the 1960s and 1970s—amplified the peaks and valleys of the baby boom and bust as measured by annual birth rates. We can obtain a more meaningful picture of the trends by examining the lifetime levels of fertility for different cohorts. The lifetime levels measure changes in the number of births over time, independent of changes in the timing of births during women's reproductive years.

Figure 1-4 displays the cohort total fertility rate for single-year birth cohorts of white and nonwhite women born between 1903 and 1956, based on data assembled by M. D. R. Evans. The cohort total fertility rate is the mean number of children born per woman in a particular cohort. For cohorts of women past their reproductive years, this rate can be calculated from survey or birth registration data; for the more recent cohorts, future levels of fertility must be estimated.[28] As the figure shows, the mean number of births per woman born in 1903 was 2.40 for whites and 2.68 for nonwhites. This level, as best we can tell, had declined throughout the nineteenth century.[29] The total fertility rate continued to decline through the cohorts of 1908 to 1910 (who came of age early in the depression) and then rose precipitously to a high of

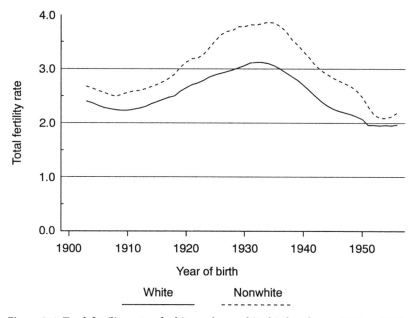

4.0

3.0

Total fertility rate

2.0

1.0

0.0

1900    1910    1920    1930    1940    1950

Year of birth

White          Nonwhite

*Figure 1-4.* Total fertility rate of white and nonwhite birth cohorts, 1903 to 1956. Source: M. D. R. Evans, "American Fertility Patterns: A Comparison of White and Nonwhite Cohorts Born 1903–56," *Population and Development Review* 12 (June 1986): 267–293.

over 3.12 for white women and 3.86 for nonwhite women born in the early 1930s (who came of age in the 1950s) before beginning a steep slide which appears to have bottomed out in the cohorts born after 1950. For the 1956 cohort, Evans estimates a total fertility rate of 1.97 for whites and 2.19 for nonwhites.[30] (I will discuss the demographic differences between whites and nonwhites in Chapter 4.)

The projections for women born in the 1950s may prove to be too low. These baby boomers did postpone childbearing when they were in their twenties, but in the 1980s they began to reach the ages at which they could no longer do so. Enough of them decided to have children so that birth rates rose 36 percent for women in their early thirties, and 26 percent for women in their late thirties, between 1980 and 1988.[31] The timing of births is now considerably later than was the case in the 1970s, and the share of all births born to older mothers is greater. In

1976, women aged 30 and older accounted for just 20 percent of all births to women over 18; but in 1988, women aged 30 and older accounted for 35 percent.[32] Nevertheless, when their reproductive years are over, the fertility rate of the baby boomers will have been far lower than that of their parents. It is too soon to predict the childbearing patterns of the third generation—the children of the baby boomers. But the oldest ones are showing the same tendency to delay having children; birth rates for women under 30 remained low and unchanging in the 1980s.[33]

Figure 1-4 demonstrates that trends in lifetime levels of childbearing in this century form a single, massive wave that peaked with the cohorts of women who married and began to bear children in the decade following World War II. This great rise in fertility is at variance with the long-term historical decline in childbearing over the past 150 years. To be sure, our sketchy knowledge of nineteenth-century fertility patterns also suggests that the fertility of the cohorts who reached adulthood during the depression was unusually low. And the fertility of the most recent cohorts also is quite low, although that seems to be in line with the longer historical decline. The more unusual phenomenon, in a long-term perspective, is the great increase in childbearing among those born during the 1920s and 1930s. Cohort trends in childbearing, like trends in age at marriage, suggest that the cohorts who grew up during the depression and the war years—not the cohorts who grew up during the postwar years—stand out as more historically distinctive.

## Marital Dissolution

No trend in American family life since World War II has received more attention or caused more concern than the rising rate of divorce. The divorce rate, however, has been rising since at least the middle of the nineteenth century. Figure 1-5 shows the number of divorces per 1,000 existing marriages (after 1920, per 1,000 married women) in every year between 1860 (the earliest year for which data are available) and 1988. These are annual measures, reflecting the particular social and economic conditions of each year. We can see, for example, that the annual rate of divorce increased temporarily after every major war: there is a slight

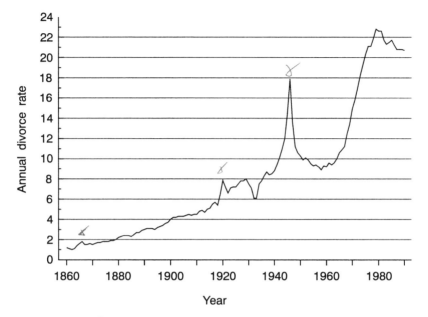

*Figure 1-5.* Annual divorce rate, United States. For 1920–1988: divorces per 1,000 married women aged 15 and over; for 1860–1920: divorces per 1,000 existing marriages. Sources: 1860–1920, Paul H. Jacobson, *American Marriage and Divorce* (New York: Rinehart, 1959), table 42; 1920–1967, U.S. National Center for Health Statistics, series 21, no. 24, *100 Years of Marriage and Divorce Statistics* (1973), table 4; 1968–1987, U.S. National Center for Health Statistics, *Monthly Vital Statistics Report*, vol. 38, no. 12, supplement 2, "Advance Report of Final Divorce Statistics, 1987," table 1; 1988, U.S. National Center for Health Statistics, *Monthly Vital Statistics Report*, vol. 38, no. 13, "Annual Summary of Births, Marriages, Divorces, and Deaths: United States, 1989."

bulge in the graph following the Civil War, a rise in 1919 and 1920 following World War I, and a large spike in the years immediately after World War II. We can also see how the depression temporarily lowered the divorce rate in the early 1930s: with jobs and housing scarce, many couples had to postpone divorcing until they could afford to do so.

Ignoring for the moment the temporary movements induced by war and depression, there is a slow, steady increase in the annual rate of divorce through the end of World War II. Since the war, however, the graph looks somewhat different. In the period from 1950 to 1960 the annual rates are lower than what we would expect on the basis of the long-term rise. Then, starting in the early 1960s, the annual rates rise sharply, so that by the end of the 1970s the rate of divorce is well above what would be predicted from the long-term trend. After peaking in 1979, the divorce rate declined slightly in the 1980s; but it is still far above the levels of the 1960s. Thus if we compare the annual rates from the 1950s with those from the 1970s and 1980s, as many observers have tended to do, we are comparing a period of relatively low rates with a time of very high rates. The result is to make the recent rise loom even larger than it would if we took the long-term view.

It is true that the rise in annual divorce rates in the 1960s and 1970s was much steeper and more sustained than any increase in the past century; but to gauge the significance of this recent rise, it is necessary to consider the lifetime divorce experiences of adults, rather than just the annual rates of divorce. In Figure 1-6 the dotted line is an estimate of the proportion of all marriages begun in every year between 1867

*Figure 1-6.* Proportion of marriages begun in each year that will end in divorce, 1867 to 1985. Sources: See notes 34 and 35.

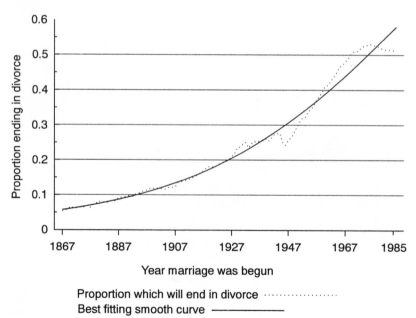

Proportion which will end in divorce ⋯⋯⋯⋯⋯⋯

Best fitting smooth curve ——————

and 1985 which have ended, or will end, in divorce before one of the spouses dies. Following conventional usage among demographers, I refer to all people marrying in a given year as a "marriage cohort." For recent marriage cohorts, the lifetime record is incomplete, and I have relied on projections prepared by Samuel H. Preston, John McDonald, and James Weed.[34] Any projection, of course, can be undermined by future events, so the importance of Figure 1-6 lies more in the general trends it shows than in its precise estimate for recent marriage cohorts. We can see from the dotted line that the proportion of all marriages in a given year that eventually end in divorce has increased at a faster and faster rate since the mid-nineteenth century. Moreover, the increase has been relatively steady, without the large fluctuations which the annual rates show in times of war or depression.

In order to make the underlying long-term trend clearer, the graph also shows the smooth curve that most closely fits the pattern of change.[35] People who married in the years when the dotted line is above the smooth curve were more likely to become divorced than the long-term historical trend would lead us to expect; people who married in years when the dotted line is below the smooth curve were less likely to become divorced than would be expected. We can see, for instance, that although the annual divorce rates were temporarily low in the early 1930s, more of the people who married just before or during the depression eventually became divorced than we would expect from the long-term trend. The hardship and distress families suffered when breadwinners lost their jobs irrevocably damaged some marriages, and many unhappy couples later divorced after economic conditions improved enough to allow them to do so. Conversely, Figure 1-6 indicates that the proportion of ever-divorced for those marrying between the end of the war and the late 1950s probably will not reach the expected levels based on the long-term trend. To be sure, a greater proportion of them will divorce than was the case for previous marriage cohorts, but the increase will be modest by historical standards.

On the other hand, for those who married in the 1960s and the 1970s, the increases are likely to exceed what would be predicted by the long-term trend. Couples who married in 1970, for instance, lived the early years of their marriage during a period of very high annual divorce rates. By 1977, only seven years after they had married, one-quarter of these couples had already divorced. In contrast, it was twenty-five years before one-quarter of those who married in 1950 had divorced. Weed projected that 51 percent of marriages begun in 1970, and 53 percent of those begun in 1976 and 1977, eventually will end in divorce.[36]

Among the most recent marriage cohorts there is yet another turn-about, as Figure 1-6 shows. If divorce rates continue to decline slightly, or even if they remain constant, couples who married in the 1980s will have lower lifetime levels of divorce than the historical record would predict. If these rates continue, the probability of ending a marriage in divorce would rest on a high plateau—Weed projects that 51 percent of 1985 marriages would end in divorce if the rates were to remain close to the level of the mid-1980s. Such a development could mark the end of more than a century of exponential increases in divorce. But it is difficult to tell whether divorce rates will remain stable or begin to rise again. In Chapter 2 I will discuss what is known about the causes of the rise in divorce; let it suffice here to say that social scientists can't predict the demographic future very well.

There are other estimates of the proportion of recent marriages that would end in divorce at current rates. At the low end, Robert Schoen estimated that 44.1 percent of married women and 43.9 percent of married men would end their marriages in divorce if recent rates continued.[37] At the high end, Teresa Castro Martin and Larry L. Bumpass, using different data, estimated that up to 64 percent of recent marriages would end in separation or divorce if recent rates continued.[38] Bumpass and Martin included marital separation, noting that about 5 percent of marriages end in separations that are not followed by a divorce. Even so, their predictions are startlingly high. Who is right? All of these demographers are making different assumptions about the future, and all are forced to use imperfect data. I think it's safe to say that about half of all marriages will end in a separation or a divorce if current rates continue.

In sum, although annual measures of divorce often show large fluc-tuations from year to year or decade to decade, the lifetime proportions ever-divorced for people marrying in a given year have risen in a regular fashion for the past century, with some variations. Those who married during the depression and those who married in the 1960s and 1970s experienced even higher levels of divorce over their lifetimes than the historical trend would predict. And those who married in the decade or so following the war were the only cohorts in the last hundred years to show a substantial, sustained shortfall in their lifetime levels of divorce. This latter group, of course, includes most of the parents of the baby boomers. Figure 1-6 suggests that the lifetime level of divorce for the baby boom parents was unusually low; for their children it will be unusually high. As for those who married in the 1980s, the incomplete record so far suggests that their levels of divorce may fall below the historical trend, but that still will leave them with a very high rate of marital disruption.

The other way in which a marriage can terminate, of course, is with the death of one spouse. Because mortality rates have declined in the twentieth century, the annual rate of death for married persons has declined at the same time that the annual rate of divorce has been rising. Some demographers have noted that, as a result, the total rate of marital dissolution—the number of marriages ending in either divorce or death in a given year per 1,000 existing marriages—hardly changed between 1860 and 1970. From 1860 to 1864 the combined rate was 33.2 dissolutions per 1,000 marriages; in 1970 the combined rate was 34.5.[39] Since 1970, however, the rising rate of divorce has pushed the total dissolution rate above its historical high. The rate peaked at about 41 in the late 1970s and early 1980s; then as divorce rates fell slightly and death rates continued to decline, it fell to 38.7 in 1989.[40] In the mid-nineteenth century, most of the dissolutions in a given year were caused by the death of one spouse, but by the mid-1970s, for the first time in our nation's history, more marriages ended every year in divorce than in death.[41]

Divorces tend to occur at a different stage of family life than deaths, and the two types of dissolution have different consequences for the remaining family members. Most people who divorce do so early in their marriage—about half of all divorces occur by the seventh year of marriage[42]—so that many divorces happen when children are still in the home. In the past, it was common for parents to die while their children were still young, but as mortality rates have fallen, a greater proportion of parental deaths have occurred when the children have already reached adulthood. Consequently, the most important effect on family life of any further fall in death rates will be to extend the "empty nest" stage of marriage after the children leave home. One of the most important effects of the rise in divorce, on the other hand, is to increase the proportion of parents whose marriage is dissolved while their children are still at home. At the rates of the early 1960s, about one-fifth of all children would have experienced the disruption of their parents' marriages before they reached sixteen, but at the rates of the late 1970s and 1980s, about two-fifths would experience a disruption by age sixteen.[43]

Most of these disruptions result, at least temporarily, in a one-parent household consisting of a mother and her children, because mothers keep custody of their children in most instances. Among all children not living with two parents in 1990, 79 percent were living with their mother, only 11 percent with their father, and most of the rest with other relatives.[44] As marital disruption increased in the 1970s, so did the number of one-parent households headed by women. In 1990, 6.6 million women headed households that included their own children under eighteen, more than double the number in 1970.[45] Earlier in the century, it was common for divorcing parents to send their children to live with relatives or for divorced mothers to take their children and move in with kin. Today, however, most currently divorced mothers live alone with their children.[46] About half of the children in one-parent households formed by marital disruption will spend five years in this type of family before their mother remarries or they turn eighteen.[47] Much has been written about the social and economic situation of parents and children in one-parent households, and I discuss the consequences of living in such a household in later chapters.

One other form of marital dissolution to be considered is separation. Most married couples stop living together before they are legally divorced. Some remain separated—without divorcing—for an extended period or even for the rest of their lives. Others separate and then reconcile their differences and resume their marriages. Even for couples who eventually divorce, the process of moving into separate households may be more difficult and traumatic than subsequently obtaining a divorce. Unfortunately, little is known about separation. Unlike marriage and divorce, which are always sanctioned by the state, many separations are informal arrangements between two spouses. Consequently, official records on legal separations, which are incomplete in any case, give an inadequate picture of the number of separations. A 1980 survey in which the Bureau of the Census asked about separation and divorce revealed that most separated people obtain a divorce quickly: 58 percent of women and 63 percent of men within one year, and 77 and 82 percent, respectively, within two years.[48] Separated black women and men, however, are much less likely to obtain a rapid divorce: only 42 percent of women and 53 percent of men were divorced within two years.[49]

## Remarriage after Divorce

Remarriages have been common in the United States since its beginnings, but until this century almost all remarriages followed widowhood. In the Plymouth Colony about one-third of all men and one-quarter of all women who lived full lifetimes remarried after the death of a spouse, but there was little divorce.[50] Even as late as the 1920s, brides and grooms who were remarrying were more likely to have been widowed than divorced.[51] Since then, however, the increase in divorce and the decline in mortality have altered the balance: by 1987, 91 percent of all brides and all grooms who were remarrying were previously divorced, and 9 percent were widowed.[52] Thus it is only since the depression that remarriage after divorce has become the predominant form of remarriage. And since the turn of the century, such remarriages have increased as a proportion of all marriages. In 1900 only 3 percent of all brides—including both the never-married and the previously married—were divorced. In 1930, 9 percent of all brides were divorced; and in 1987, 32 percent of all brides were divorced.[53]

In the early 1960s, when the divorce rate began to rise sharply, the remarriage rate for divorced people also rose. This parallel rise was taken to mean that Americans still embraced the institution of marriage, even though many were rejecting their current spouses. In the 1970s, however, while the divorce rate still soared, the remarriage rate fell—and it remained low and relatively stable in the 1980s.[54] Yet we now know that separated and divorced adults were as likely to be living with new partners in the mid-1980s as in 1970—they just weren't as likely to have married them. The National Survey of Families and Households revealed that although there was a 16 percent drop between 1970 and 1984 in the proportion of separated and divorced adults who remarried within five years, there was a 7 percent *increase* in the proportion who formed a union—either by cohabiting or marrying—within five years.[55] In fact, as noted earlier, cohabitation before remarriage is even more common than cohabitation before first marriage: 60 percent of persons who remarried between 1980 and 1987 lived with someone before the marriage—46 percent with only the person they married and 14 percent with someone else.[56]

So union formation after a marital separation is occurring at the same speed as, or even a bit faster than, twenty years ago. The majority of these first unions of divorced people are cohabiting unions. Separated and divorced adults may be rejecting rapid remarriage, but they aren't rejecting living with a partner. And most eventually remarry—about two-thirds of divorced women and three-fourths of divorced men.[57] Blacks, however, are much less likely to make the transition to remarriage than are whites. Only 32 percent of black women and 55 percent of black men remarry within ten years.[58]

When either partner in a remarriage has children from a previous marriage, the structure of the new family can be quite complex. It may include children from the wife's previous marriages, from the husband's previous marriages, and from the new marriage. The children from previous marriages often create links between the household of the remarried parent and the household of that parent's ex-spouse. Stepgrandparents and other quasi-kin may play important roles in the lives of the parents and children. Not all families of remarriage, of course, exhibit the full range of complexity. Still, according to the NSFH, one out of every seven children in a two-parent family was living with a parent and a stepparent.[59]

Conventional wisdom suggests that remarriages should be more successful than first marriages because of the greater maturity and experience of the partners, but the divorce statistics suggest otherwise.

During the first several years of marriage, the rate of divorce for remarriages is substantially higher than for first marriages; afterward, the rates are similar. By one estimate, 37 percent of remarriages among women end in a separation or a divorce within ten years, compared to 30 percent of first marriages.[60] Some researchers have linked this higher probability of divorce to the complex family structures of remarriages, while others have argued that the first-married and remarried populations differ in personal characteristics that could influence the risk of divorce. In either case, the expanded families of remarriage after divorce may complicate the lives of remarried adults and their children.

In attempting to summarize the changes in marriage, divorce, and remarriage since World War II, it is important to choose our frame of reference with care. We often contrast the situation of the 1950s with that of the 1970s and 1980s, implicitly assuming that the 1950s were representative of family life throughout the first half of the century. Thus we sometimes conclude that the family patterns of the 1970s and 1980s differ sharply overall from what was experienced in the past. But as I have shown in this chapter, this conclusion is too broad; in many respects it is the 1950s that stand out as more unusual.

During that decade the men and women born and raised during the depression and the war years came of age. They married sooner than any other cohorts who have reached adulthood in the twentieth century before or since. About three-fourths of the women born in 1930 to 1934 were married by age twenty-three; in contrast, women born twenty years earlier or later were two or three years older before three-fourths of them had married. Moreover, the long-term rise in divorce affected those who came of age in the 1950s less than some other cohorts. In addition, more of the women in the parental generation of the 1950s had two or more children than did the women in either their parents' or their children's generations. The distinctive family patterns of the young adults of the 1950s suggest that when we look for explanations of the postwar trends, we should examine the experience of growing up in the depression and the war years.

As for the children of the parental generation of the 1950s—who were born during the baby boom and who reached adulthood in the

1960s and 1970s—they, too, have been distinctive in some respects. To be sure, their pattern of marrying has been more like the typical twentieth-century pattern than was the case for their parents' generation. But in the 1980s, women's average age at marriage rose beyond the previous twentieth-century high. And since about 1970 there has been a great increase in cohabitation prior to and after marriages. These recent changes suggest that the place of the institution of marriage in American society may be changing.

Moreover, the lifetime levels of divorce for persons who married in the 1960s and 1970s will increase beyond what we would expect from the long-term trend. Rates in the 1980s, although stable, still imply that about half of all the marriages begun in the mid-1970s will end in divorce or separation. Most of those who divorce will live with a partner and eventually marry, creating an unprecedented number of unions in which one or both partners has been previously married.

# 2

# Explanations

Each change in family life since the depression seems to have taken scholars by surprise. The dismal employment situation of the 1930s forced single people to postpone marrying and forced married couples to postpone having children. Worried experts warned that the low rate of births, if sustained, would lead to a drastic decrease in population. In 1933 a presidential panel predicted that the American population would peak at between 145 and 190 million and then decline.[1] In 1990 it was about 250 million and still rising. Even as late as the end of World War II, respected demographers were sticking to their pessimistic projections.

What no one foresaw was the postwar baby boom. The young men and women of the late 1940s and 1950s married earlier and had children faster than did their parents' generation. Then in the 1960s the divorce rate began to rise very steeply, fertility fell once again, and young adults again postponed marrying. Although there are many explanations for these ups and downs, most can be classified as either "period" or "cohort" explanations. Partisans of the former emphasize society-wide shifts that appear to affect all groups at the same time, as if there were something in the air that influenced everyone's lives.[2] Period explanations for the postwar changes in the family identify swings in attitudes and values, from the focus on family of the fifties to the individualism of the seventies and eighties, or swings in economic conditions from boom to bust. The family-centered values and the postwar prosperity of the 1950s, according to this view, encouraged young adults to marry and to begin having children earlier. Then the shift in the 1970s toward a more individualistic ethos and the economic stagnation after the oil price shock of 1973 discouraged early marriage and childbearing.

Partisans of cohort explanations emphasize the distinctiveness of a particular birth cohort, particularly the distinctive conditions under which they grew up. One of the most important is simply the cohort's size. When a small cohort reaches adulthood, there are fewer workers to fill job openings, and wages are likely to rise; the opposite can happen when a large cohort enters the work force. Those who favor cohort explanations for the postwar era argue that the small size of the depression cohort ensured that the wages of workers in the 1950s would be high, whereas the large size of the baby boom cohort meant that wages would stagnate. Furthermore, they argue that people who grew up during the depression had low expectations for material goods and craved a secure and stable family life. Therefore, according to this line of reasoning, young adults in the 1950s used rising earnings to marry earlier and have children sooner.

These two perspectives correspond to two general types of explanation for change over time in human behavior. Since each cohort lives in a different period and therefore is subject to a different set of period-based influences, it is difficult to determine whether social change from generation to generation is produced by the differing characteristics of the cohorts involved or by society-wide changes during the time period studied. Period-based and cohort-based effects, in other words, are often confounded.[3]

Nevertheless, it is clear from the vantage point of the 1990s that period effects have dominated trends in marriage, divorce, and childbearing in this century. Figure 2-1 shows the probability of having a first birth or marrying for the first time for white women, from 1917 until the 1980s. (The patterns for blacks were similar until the mid-1960s; the divergence since then will be discussed in Chapter 4.) When the probability of having a birth or getting married dropped in the 1930s, it dropped for all women, whether in their twenties or thirties. When it peaked just after World War II, it peaked for everyone. By and large, the lines move in parallel, meaning that in a period when the birth or marriage rate was low it was low for all, and when it was high it was high for all. A graph of divorce probabilities would show the same pattern.[4] It is the pattern one would expect if similar forces were affecting everyone at the same time, regardless of their age—that is, regardless of their birth cohort. This pattern implies period effects.[5]

There are some exceptions that suggest cohort effects. The top panel

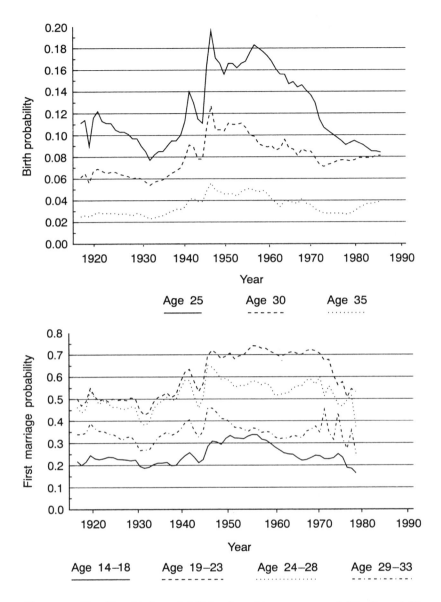

*Figure 2-1. Top,* First birth probabilities for white women aged 25, 30, and 35, 1917–1986. Sources: Ronald R. Rindfuss, S. Philip Morgan, and Gray Swicegood, *First Births in America* (Berkeley: University of California Press, 1988); and Renbao Chen and S. Philip Morgan, "Recent Trends in Timing of First Birth in the United States," *Demography* 4 (November 1991): 513–533. *Bottom,* Five-year first marriage probabilities for white women at ages 14–18, 19–23, 24–28, and 29–33, for 1917–1979. Source: Willard R. Rodgers and Arland Thornton, "Changing Pattern of First Marriage in the United States," *Demography* 22 (May 1985): 265–279.

shows that birth probabilities for 25-year-old women (the highest line) rose to a second peak in the late 1950s, but births to older women did not. During the same period, marriages to women age 19 to 23 (bottom panel, highest line) remained high even though marriages to older women began to drop. So the figure does suggest that there may have been some circumstances leading to early marriage and childbearing that were unique to the cohort of women who reached early adulthood in the 1950s, at the height of the baby boom. And since 1980, as the top panel shows, birth probabilities have risen for women in their thirties but not for younger women. So something about the history of the cohort of women now in their thirties—undoubtedly their unprecedented postponement of having children—is making their current behavior distinctive.

It is easy to look at graphs such as these and decide that most of the story lies in period effects, but it is much harder to determine what those period effects were. And it is easier to pick out a few upturns that look like cohort effects than to specify what made the curves turn up. There is much disagreement among scholars about the causes of the trends. The disagreement is strongest concerning the 1950s, the most unusual decade.

## The 1950s

After nearly a decade of depression and four terrible years of war, Americans finally achieved prosperity as they entered the 1950s. And, except for the more limited Korean conflict, they finally had peace. Millions of men and women had been forced to postpone marrying during the hard times of the 1930s and the austerity and separation brought about by the war. It was not surprising, then, that they married in record numbers in the late 1940s and that the birth rate soon rose dramatically. What was surprising was that years after this pent-up demand for marriage and children should have been satisfied, the birth and marriage rates remained high. As late as 1956, the Bureau of the Census estimated that nearly half of all young women who would ever marry would do so before they reached age twenty.[6] Moreover, the annual birth rate rose steadily in the 1950s, reaching its peak in 1957.

Had the birth rate remained at the 1957 level, the average woman would have given birth to four children before the end of her childbearing years.[7] (In fact, the birth rate fell sharply in the 1960s and 1970s.)

Nowhere was the increased emphasis on home and family more noticeable than in the expanding suburbs. With the help of government-guaranteed mortgages, millions of families purchased single-family homes beyond the borders of the cities. The family-centered life in the suburbs came under sharp attack from social critics as bland, conformist, and overly centered on women and children. The long commute to work, they said, kept husbands away from early in the morning until night. Meanwhile, the mothers supposedly were engaged in an endless round of activities on behalf of their children, chauffeuring them to nursery school, ballet lessons, and Little League games.[8]

Yet the move to a single-family suburban house represented for millions a great leap forward into the middle class. In suburb and city, families were experiencing dramatic increases in their standard of living. Fifty years later, we tend to forget how much lower the average standard of living was in the mid-1940s: one-third of all homes did not have running water, two-fifths did not have flush toilets, half did not have electric refrigerators. Then the postwar economic boom began, and median family income, adjusted for inflation, increased by 42 percent in the 1950s and another 38 percent in the 1960s.[9] The relative affluence allowed young families to form earlier and to have two or three children in short order without sacrificing the goal of a comfortable life.

Yet affluence alone couldn't have caused the baby boom; in the decade after World War I Americans' standard of living also increased, although more modestly, but the birth rate continued to fall.[10] It seems quite likely, consequently, that the spread of family-centered values played an important role in the baby boom. We know from European historical studies that the spread of new values and ideas can bring about rapid changes in birth rates. In European provinces, birth rates often remained high, even after the growth of wage labor, until the spread of new ideas and values triggered a rapid decline. The declines occurred piecemeal, province by province as values diffused across local language barriers and trade markets.[11] But in the contemporary United States, with its common language, national media, and integrated market, it is reasonable to think that a change could be triggered simultaneously throughout the country.[12]

This is not to say that Americans didn't value their family lives before 1950 but rather that there was an increasing emphasis during the 1950s on marriage and parenthood as central to a fulfilling life. Nearly all accounts of the 1950s stress the great importance attached to home, family, and children. Many popular commentators ascribed this shift to what they saw as a great national exhaustion: emotionally drained from their earlier battles against economic collapse and foreign enemies, Americans supposedly shunned the great issues of the day and retreated into their personal lives.[13] Indeed, widely read authors and commentators and well-known political leaders in the 1950s all extolled the virtues of a traditional family life. Women's magazines published a steady stream of articles praising the homemaker and warning women of the perils of trying to combine marriage and childrearing with work outside the home. Adlai Stevenson, the great liberal of the day, addressed the graduates of Smith College in 1955 and advised them that their place in politics was to "influence man and boy" through the "humble role of housewife."

National exhaustion seems insufficient, however, to explain a phenomenon that lasted nearly twenty years. Sociologist Randall Collins argues that the rising standard of living allowed for the flowering of working-class culture. As blue-collar workers bought suburban homes, they brought with them a style of life, Collins maintains, that was more group-oriented, more family-centered, and less individualistic.[14] Collins's point, that the upper-middle-class cultural critics failed to see the working-class roots of many suburban residents, is well taken. But the kinds of families the new suburbanites created were unlike the working-class model. The distinctive characteristics of working-class families are greater emphasis on ties to a network of kin, lesser emphasis on marital closeness, adult-centeredness, and higher value on obedience in childrearing.[15] In contrast, the families celebrated in the media and constructed in the suburbs were isolated, child-centered families with a heavy emotional investment in the husband-wife bond.[16] They were breadwinner-homemaker families—the self-sufficient, emotionally intense, child-oriented middle-class ideal in which the wife ran the home and the husband earned the money.[17] This was the idea that spread through the suburbs. Attaining this style of family life was the goal of the millions of newly prosperous homeowners.

It is still not clear why the breadwinner-homemaker family became such a powerful ideal in the 1950s. Perhaps it was the unattainable style to which many aspired during the difficult years of the depression and the war, and which they rushed to achieve as soon as they had the means to do so. The demographer Ron Lesthaeghe argues that the Allied victory produced a renewed faith in public institutions, a renewed confidence in the stability of the democratic state that allowed people to build families.[18] On the other hand, historian Elaine Tyler May argues that the uneasy Cold War peace undermined confidence in the future and led people to retreat to the safety of home and family.[19]

In either case, the heyday of the breadwinner-homemaker family concealed contradictions that led to its rapid demise after the mid-1960s. At the same time that the media were promoting single-earner family values, more and more married women were taking jobs outside the home. As the service sector of the economy expanded, demand increased and wages rose for workers in what had become typed as female occupations. These were relatively low-paying jobs that nevertheless required some education—secretary, telephone operator, elementary school teacher. Earlier in the century these posts had been filled by single women who were expected to quit when they married, or certainly as soon as they were pregnant. In the 1950s, better opportunities drew more and more married women back into the work force.

The higher birth rates concealed a long-term change in the value of having children. When children could be put to work on the farm at age five or sent to toil at ten in factories, they were an economic asset to their parents. Since the nineteenth century children have needed an ever longer, ever more expensive period of training before entering the labor force. The training period lengthened significantly after World War II with the growth of college education. Between 1940 and 1960, the proportion of young adults with a college degree doubled.[20] As the period of training lengthened, children, in strict financial terms, became more of a cost than an asset to parents. To be sure, the emotional satisfaction parents derive from their children remained—and perhaps even increased. But given the cost, the strategy of parents shifted from having many children and putting them to work to having one or two or possibly three children and investing heavily in their development.

Parents, in other words, began to trade quantity for quality. This shift was missed by the many commentators in the 1950s who talked about the four- or five-child family as if families this large had once again become common. We now know that there was not a return to large families in the 1950s. Much of the increase in the annual birth rates can be traced to two developments: a greater proportion of young women had at least two children, and women tended to have their children sooner after they married. There was also an increase in the proportion of women who had three or four children, but there appears to have been a decrease in the proportion who had more than four.[21] The decline of large families presaged a decline in two-child families later in the century.

Moreover, the family values of the 1950s contained elements of a more individualistic ethos that would help transform family life again a generation later. Under that ethos, which has gained force throughout the West since the emergence of commercial capitalism, individuals increasingly have sought meaning in life through self-fulfillment and intimacy.[22] The family form celebrated in the 1950s was the isolated nuclear family consisting of only parents and children. It fit the ethos by providing a more private setting for personal life—an escape from grandparents, uncles, aunts, and other kin. As bonds to a wider network of kin weakened, the relationship between husbands and wives became highly charged emotionally and sexually. A person's satisfaction came from intimate relations with his or her spouse and from the gratification of raising children together. But there is no reason why individualism should stop with the nuclear family—after all, obligations to spouses and children can conflict with personal desires as well. Since the mid-1960s, the quest for self-fulfillment and intimacy has taken an even more individualistic tone; increasingly, what counts most is one's own emotional satisfaction, even if it clashes with the needs of spouses and children and even if it leads to the break-up of a marriage. Although the pre-1965 and post-1965 versions of this ethos had very different consequences for marriage and childbearing, an underlying current of individualism and intimacy linked them.[23]

So far I have emphasized period explanations for the trends observed in the 1950s. But, as I noted, the levels of early marriage and childbearing did seem particularly high for the cohort that reached young adulthood at the height of the baby boom in the mid-to-late 1950s. There is reason to believe that their behavior in the 1950s was in part due to their childhood and adolescent experiences during the 1930s. Growing up in the depression often meant belonging to a family in which the father was unable to find steady work—or, in many cases, any work at all. When the father was unemployed, the family's income plummeted, and wives and teenage children, especially teenage boys, were forced to get a job if they could. A man who had been a reliable breadwinner before the depression might watch helplessly as his wife and children became the family's only wage earners. In this situation the father lost not only his income but also his authority. Mirra Komarovsky reported on the breakdown of the unemployed father's status at home in her classic study, *The Unemployed Man and His Family.* She wrote about one man who had been on relief for three years:

> Mr. Brady says that while the children don't blame him for his unemployment, he is sure that they don't think as much about the old man as they used to. "It's only natural. When a father cannot support his family, supply them with clothing and good food, the children are bound to lose respect."[24]

Mr. Brady's seventeen-year-old son Henry was the only employed member of the family, earning $12 per week. He told Komarovsky:

> "I'm my own boss now. Nobody can tell me what to do or how to spend my money. Working makes you feel independent. I remind them who makes the money. They don't say much. They just take it, that's all. I'm not the one on relief. I can't help feeling that way."
>
> Henry said that seeing his father so discouraged and without ambition made him lose respect for him. "He is not the same father, that's all. You can't help not looking up to him like we used to."[25]

Once, when the family was almost finished with dinner, Henry walked in. There were no extra chairs, so Mr. Brady got up and relinquished his seat to his son. Henry took his father's place at the table in a matter-of-fact way, as if it were his due.

Did the experiences of Henry Brady and other adolescents from homes hit hard by the depression influence their later patterns of marriage and family life? One scholar who has addressed this question is sociologist Glen H. Elder, Jr. His study of children born in Oakland, California, in 1920 and 1921, *Children of the Great Depression,* traces the long-term effects of the depression on some of the children who grew up during it.[26] The Oakland Growth Study, as it was originally called, was begun in 1932 as a study of the physical, intellectual, and social development of 167 children who were then eleven years old. The researchers reinterviewed these subjects periodically until the mid-1960s. Elder divided the subjects into middle-class and working-class groups, and he also divided them into "deprived" and "nondeprived" groups.[27]

Elder demonstrated how independence increased during the depression and explored its consequences for adolescent boys. When Oakland families were hit by the depression, teenage sons were sent to work to help compensate for their fathers' lost earnings. The sons' incomes increased their independence from parental control, as Komarovsky showed in the case of Henry Brady, and their jobs gave the boys a chance to extend their network of friends and acquaintances. They often became more actively involved with their peers, they went out on school nights, they dated earlier. Because many mothers had to find paid employment, their daughters were required to help more around the house. Consequently, at an early age girls became heavily involved with the tasks that make up the traditional adult female role of homemaker or housewife. Elder characterized the overall experiences of the deprived boys and girls during the 1930s as "the downward extension of adultlike experience." Boys became more involved in the kind of work adult males typically did, and girls took on more of the work adult women typically did.

Most of the Oakland children married during or just after the war and had their first child soon thereafter. Women from economically deprived families, Elder found, married earlier and placed a higher value on family activities—as opposed to work, leisure, or community activities—than did women from the nondeprived families. In general, family life was more highly valued among those Oakland men and women whose families had suffered most from the effects of the depression while they were growing up. Perhaps, as Elder suggested, these children of the depression came to view strong families as valuable resources that were all the more desirable because of their scarcity during the years of economic hardship. Or perhaps children were seen as a wise investment by men and women who had seen their own parents subsist only with the aid of the money that children brought home. Whatever the precise mechanism, the Oakland study strongly suggests that the experience of growing up in a deprived family during the depression influenced the attitudes of men and women toward marriage, family, and children.

Elder and other sociologists who have studied depression life have emphasized the social and psychological effects of economic hardship; the economist Richard A. Easterlin has also considered the demographic effects.[28] As I described above, the birth rate dropped during the 1920s and then plunged even lower during the depression, to the point that some eminent demographers predicted that the United States population would soon decline. The relatively small size of the cohorts born in the 1920s and 1930s at first made little difference in their lives; but, according to Easterlin, this factor was later a distinct advantage. For, as it turned out, these men and women had the good fortune to begin to marry and to have children in the late 1940s and the 1950s, when the American economy started its sustained postwar boom. The demand for young workers was high, and because of the small size of these cohorts, the supply was low. This imbalance made it easier for young adult males to find a satisfactory job. By and large, their earnings were high compared to those of young men during the depression.

Even the relatively good employment picture in the 1950s, though, didn't necessarily ensure that couples would marry younger and that births would increase. It could have happened, Easterlin points out, that single young men would spend their larger paychecks on themselves and that young couples would use all of their extra money to buy bigger houses, more furniture, and the like. That they didn't do so, he contends, was the result of one of the psychological effects of growing up in the depression. A person's standard of living, Easterlin maintains, is determined by the material conditions he or she experiences during childhood and especially during adolescence. Consequently the children who grew up during the scarcity of the depression developed a modest taste for material goods. When they reached adulthood, the favorable employment situation for young men meant that they could marry, satisfy their desires for material goods, and still have money left over to cover the costs of having and raising children. Thus their relatively favorable employment situation, in conjunction with the modest material standards these men and their wives developed while growing up, resulted in a trend toward earlier marriage and more childbearing. In addition, the same favorable situation led to less conflict between spouses and a smaller rise in the divorce rate than the long-term trend would have indicated.

At least one difficulty arises when we use these cohort-based explanations to account for the trends of the 1950s. As Elder's study suggests, and as Easterlin has noted, the psychological impact of the depression probably was stronger for adolescents than for younger children. Komarovsky made a similar distinction: many of the unemployed fathers in her sample appeared to lose authority over their teenaged children, but they were more likely to report an improvement than a deterioration in their relationship with children under twelve.[29] Those who were teenagers during the depression years, of course, had to have been born by the early 1920s. It is unlikely that the lives of children born in the 1930s—who reached adolescence after the war—were touched by the depression in the same way as the Oakland cohort of 1920–1921. The cohorts of the 1930s were too young to have shared fully in the downward extension of adultlike experience, and they may have been too young to have had their standard of living influenced by the hardship around them. Thus we cannot easily extend Elder's analysis to the men and women born in the 1930s, nor can we assume that they developed a modest taste for material goods. Yet when the cohorts of the 1930s reached adulthood in the mid-to-late 1950s they continued, and even advanced, the trend toward earlier marriage and childbearing.

Elder's study of men and women born in the early 1920s, therefore, helps us to understand the behavior of only some members of the parental generation of the 1950s. Easterlin's model also works better for people who were born in the 1920s than for those born in the 1930s. Still, an important part of Easterlin's model does apply more generally: both the 1920s and the 1930s cohorts were small in size; in fact, the number of births was lower in the early and mid-1930s than in the 1920s. If relative cohort size influenced the marriage and childbearing pattern of young adults independent of their material aspirations, then Easterlin's explanation may apply to most of the new parents of the 1950s.

It may well be that accounting for the trends of the 1950s requires giving credence to both period and cohort explanations. I would argue that period effects were more important but that cohort effects also were operating. The two effects reinforced each other, thus strengthening the trends of the 1950s. The childhood and adolescent experiences of many of the men and women born in the 1920s predisposed them to place a greater value on home and family and, possibly, a lower value on material comforts; when the general shift in values about family life occurred in the 1950s, they may have been in the vanguard. Moreover, the small size of the cohorts of the 1920s and 1930s worked to their advantage during the postwar economic boom. Their relatively favorable economic situation, in turn, may have made it easier for them to achieve the kind of family life they desired.

## The 1960s and 1970s

If prosperity had been the only engine driving the trends of the 1950s, then early marriage, high birth rates, and moderate divorce rates should have continued throughout the almost equally prosperous 1960s. Instead, a sharp reversal began in the middle of the decade and continued through the 1970s. In explaining this reversal, some observers stress the effects of the increase in married women who worked outside the home, others point to the tougher economic situation that young men faced in the 1970s, others note improvements in contraception, and still others write about the decline of traditional attitudes toward women's roles, marriage, and divorce. It is difficult either to reject any of these explanations out of hand or to give any of them full credit for producing the recent trends.

First, is there anything to explain? So far, I have emphasized the distinctiveness of family life in the 1950s. By extension, one could argue that the reversals of those trends in the 1960s represented a return to the usual historical pattern: young adults once again married later, the divorce rate resumed its long-term rise, and the birth rate resumed its long-term fall. This line of reasoning, carried to it logical conclusion, might suggest that there is no need to explain the trends of the 1960s and 1970s at all, except in terms of modernization, the growth and development of capitalist societies, or some such long-term perspective. Many demographers, in fact, do argue that the declining birth rate of the 1960s and 1970s should be thought of as consistent with long-term developments in our society. For example, Charles F. Westoff wrote:

> Every time the birthrate records a new low (frequently in recent years) a demographer receives inquiries from journalists about what the decline can be attributed to: "the pill," abortion, sterilization, recession, the women's movement or some other ad hoc explanation. To ask what caused the latest decline, however, is to ask the wrong question. The decline is the long-term reality. The birthrate has been coming down more or less steadily for the past 200 years in this country—with the exception of one period. The real question, and the more perplexing one, is what caused that exception: the baby boom that lasted for more than a decade after World War II.[30]

The view that the 1960s and 1970s represented a return to more typical patterns of marriage and childbearing, although contrary to conventional wisdom, does help us understand some of the recent developments in family life. Even in the 1950s, as I noted earlier, the number of large families declined as parents adopted the strategy of having two, sometimes three, and only occasionally four children and investing heavily in each of them. By the 1960s, when it was taken for granted that teenagers would graduate from high school and when large numbers continued on to college, it became clearer how long and expensive that investment could be. People came to believe that the emotional rewards of childrearing could be attained by focusing time and effort on one or two.

Yet merely noting that long-term patterns reappeared will not suffice as an explanation of all that has occurred. The indicators reviewed in Chapter 1 showed that in the 1960s and 1970s the timing of first marriage did become more consistent with the patterns prevalent before World War II. If we look ahead to the 1980s, however, we find that age at marriage continued to climb. For women it is now at the highest level in this century. And even though the timing of marriage for men is still consistent with the timing in the earlier decades of the century, the reasons why men—and women—now marry at an older age may differ from the reasons why they did so in the early 1900s. Moreover, Chapter 1 showed that the rise in divorce in the 1960s and 1970s exceeded the increase we would expect on the basis of the long-term trend over the past hundred years; it cannot be accounted for simply by appealing to the march of history.

We need to examine more specific explanations for recent developments, especially for the one that has caused the most concern, the rise in divorce. One explanation is that in recent years people have become more tolerant of divorce, making it easier for persons in unhappy marriages to leave their spouses. According to this view, much of the stigma previously associated with being a divorced person has faded; a divorce is no longer seen as a mark of failure or disgrace. Consequently, married persons are said to be more likely to resort to divorce than they were a few decades ago.

It appears, however, that attitudes toward divorce did not begin to change noticeably until about 1970, whereas the sharp upturn in divorce rates began in the early-to-mid-1960s (see Figure 1-5). In 1945 and again in 1966, national samples of adults were asked if they thought that the divorce laws in their states were too strict or not strict enough. As Figure 2-2 demonstrates, the most popular response in 1945 was "not strict enough," and virtually the same proportion of people gave this response in 1966 as in 1945. In addition, there was a modest four-percentage-point increase in those saying "too strict" between 1945 and 1966, but the largest changes were a decrease in those saying "about right" and an increase in those saying they didn't know. These results

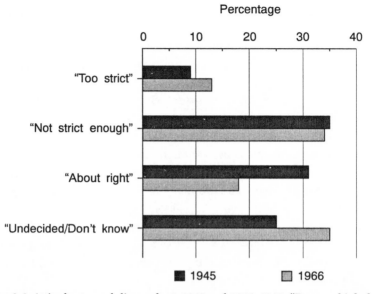

*Figure 2-2.* Attitudes toward divorce laws, 1945 and 1966. 1945: "Do you think the divorce laws in your state are now too strict or not strict enough?" 1966: "Generally speaking, would you say divorce laws in this state are too strict or not strict enough?" Sources: American Institute of Public Opinion, Study 341 (1945) and 723 (1966). 1945 data published in "The Quarter's Polls," *Public Opinion Quarterly* 9 (Summer 1945): 223. 1966 data published in Gallup Opinion Index, report no. 9 (February 1966), p. 21.

suggest that between 1945 and 1966 attitudes toward divorce changed slowly, although there may have been fluctuations during the intervening two decades that these two surveys cannot reflect.

Sometime after 1968, however, there was a sharp change in attitudes. In 1968, 1974, 1982, and 1989, national samples of adults were asked if they thought that divorce in this country should be easier or more difficult to obtain than it is now. Between 1968 and 1974, as Figure 2-3 shows, the percentage responding "easier" rose by 15 percentage points and the percentage responding "more difficult" dropped by 21 percentage points. Thus, sometime between 1968 and 1974 more adults began to favor the easier granting of divorce. By the early 1980s, however, the percentage responding "easier" had fallen, and the proportion responding "more difficult" had risen correspondingly. By the end of the 1980s, a majority of Americans once again felt that divorce should be more difficult to obtain. So attitudes toward divorce laws were most favorable to liberalization around the middle of the 1970s.[31] The changes since 1974 don't necessarily indicate a hardening of attitudes toward divorce; rather, they may reflect people's responses to the introduction in the 1970s and 1980s of no-fault divorce laws throughout the country, which did make divorce easier to obtain.

It seems likely, then, that changes in attitudes toward divorce followed changes in divorce behavior. I suspect that changes in attitudes were not an important cause of the initial rise in divorce in the 1960s and, in fact, that the rise in divorce may have prompted people to begin to reassess their attitudes. That is what appears to have happened to a

*Figure 2-3.* Attitudes toward divorce, 1968, 1974, 1982, and 1989: "Should divorce in this country be easier or more difficult to obtain than it is now?" (percentages for all who gave an opinion). Sources: for 1968, American Institute for Public Opinion, Study 764, data published in Gallup Opinion Index, report no. 41, (November 1968); for 1974, 1982, and 1989, National Opinion Research Center, General Social Surveys.

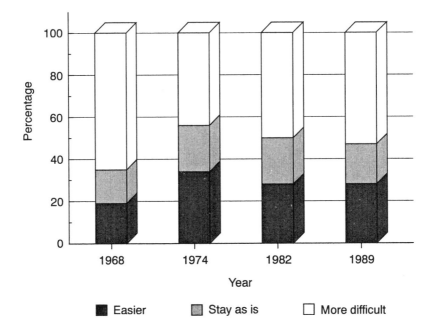

sample of about 900 young, white mothers who were interviewed several times between 1962 and 1977 by sociologists from the University of Michigan. In 1962, half of the women agreed with the statement, "When there are children in the family, parents should stay together even if they don't get along." But women who agreed with the statement were nearly as likely to dissolve their marriages during the next fifteen years as were women who disagreed; their attitudes didn't affect the likelihood of divorce. In contrast, divorce affected their attitudes: in 1977, women who had separated or divorced were much more likely to disagree with the same statement.[32]

Once attitudes toward divorce began to change markedly—probably at the start of the 1970s, give or take a few years—then the shift in people's beliefs may have provided a new stimulus for further rises in divorce. But if we are seeking an initial force behind the recent rise in divorce, we should look elsewhere. More than half of the states enacted some form of no-fault divorce legislation in the 1970s, beginning with California in 1970.[33] These laws, which make the process of divorcing easier and less stigmatizing, are another indication of the recent liberalization of attitudes toward divorce. Some observers suggested that the changes in the law would spur even more couples to divorce, but divorce statistics by state for the 1970s do not support this contention. Divorce rates in most no-fault states were no higher in the 1970s than would be expected from the trend in the states that did not reform their laws.[34] The spread of no-fault divorce laws seems to have been a reaction to changing attitudes and to the increase in divorce, not a stimulus to more divorce.

A more promising line of inquiry centers on the changes in women's roles. One of the long-term trends that scholars associate with advanced industrial societies is an increase in the proportion of married women who are employed outside the home. In the United States the employment of married women rose sharply after World War II. Since the 1960s the greatest increase has occurred among younger married women, who are subject to a greater risk of divorce than are older women. (Half of all divorces occur within about seven years of marriage.[35]) The parallel increases in the employment of younger married women and in divorce since 1960 suggest the possibility of a cause-and-effect relationship. Of course, the parallel movement of these trends could be coincidental, or both trends could be the result of some other development.

Social scientists study changes in the composition of the labor force, defined as all persons who are either employed or looking for work. By this definition, housewives are excluded from the labor force, even though they do productive work at home. Between 1900 and 1940 the percentage of all women who were in the labor force increased gradually, but since 1940 the percentage has risen dramatically. The rise has been especially pronounced for married women. In 1940 only one out of seven women who were currently married (with their husbands present) were working outside the home or looking for work; by 1979 one out of two were working or looking for work.[36] The corresponding figure for 1989 was 58 percent.[37] The change was greater for married women with children—the group that had been least likely to work—than for those without children. Figure 2-4 charts the labor force participation rates for married women with children in the postwar period. Since the mid-1960s the rate of increase has been greatest for women with preschool children. Between 1949 and 1959 the rate for married women with preschool children rose from 11 to 19 percent. By 1979 it had risen to 43 percent, and by 1989 it had risen to 58 percent.

A detailed discussion of the explanations that have been proposed for the movement of married women into the labor force would be beyond the scope of this book. In brief, many economists believe that the increase was caused by a postwar rise in women's wages, which increased the cost of staying home—namely, forgone earnings—to the point that many more wives sought paying jobs. According to this argument, older women, whose children already were in school, were drawn into the labor force first. Then a further rise in wages during the 1960s attracted increasing numbers of younger women who were caring for preschool children.[38] The sociologist Valerie K. Oppenheimer argues that the postwar rise in the number of working women was fueled by an increase in demand for workers in the service sector of the economy, where many jobs had come to be defined as women's work. More female workers were needed to fill these jobs as teachers, secretaries, nurses, and so forth, especially with the shortage of young men in the 1950s.[39]

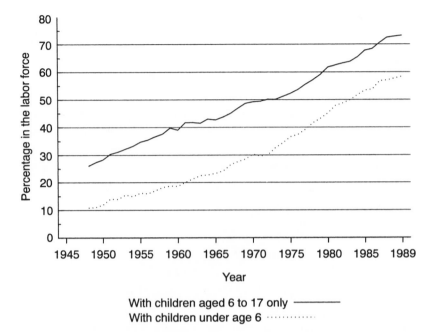

*Figure 2-4.* Labor force participation rates for married women with children, by age of children, 1948–1989. Sources: for 1948–1977, U.S. Bureau of Labor Statistics, *Handbook of Labor Statistics,* 1978, bulletin 2000 (1979); for 1978–1989, U.S. Bureau of the Census, *Statistical Abstract of the United States,* 1980, 1985, and 1991 volumes.

Richard Easterlin believes the rise to be yet another manifestation of the effects of relative cohort size.[40]

More important for our purposes than the causes of the rise in the female labor force are the possible effects of this development on marital formation and dissolution. Ever since the late nineteenth century, it has been common for single young women to work for pay outside their parents' homes. When Dreiser's Sister Carrie boarded a train for Chicago in 1889 to live with her sister and to look for a job, she was acting like many of her contemporaries. For single women employment was not, in general, a barrier to marriage; but it was expected that when a working woman found a husband, she would quit her job. Since this pattern persisted for decades, it is difficult to argue today that the mere fact of working will lead a young woman to delay marrying. A working woman might even amass a dowry of sorts, and her experience might increase her future earnings potential; either of these occurrences might make her a more desirable marriage partner. Many of the single young women who are not working today are in school, and until they finish their education, they may be less likely to marry than working women.

But although employment by itself does not delay marriage, the changing circumstances associated with young women's employment might have an effect. Better job opportunities might make marriage relatively less attractive to some working women, and they might wait longer before deciding to look seriously for a spouse. In fact, two studies of 1960 census data showed that fewer women had married in areas of the country where job opportunities for women were better, as measured by the demand in the area for jobs usually filled by women (Washington's demand was high because of its clerical work; Pittsburgh's was low because of its factory work) and by the ratio of female to male earnings.[41]

Another possibility is that, as a result of the rise in labor force participation for older married women, young single women today are more likely to believe they will be working later in life. This expectation might lead some women—especially the more educated ones—to postpone marrying while they invest time establishing themselves in the work world. I found some evidence for this hypothesis in a national sample of single women in their late teens and early twenties who were first interviewed in the late 1960s or early 1970s, then reinterviewed two years later. Other things being equal, whether a woman was working at the time of the first interview made little or no difference for whether she had married two years later. But women who said at the first interview that they planned to work at age thirty-five were, in general, less likely to have married two years later. During the period in which the study took place—1969 to 1975—the proportion of young single women who planned to work at age thirty-five rose dramatically, especially among those with more education. Perhaps this change in expectations led some of these women to postpone marrying.[42]

As for the rise in divorce and separation, almost every well-known scholar who has addressed this topic in the twentieth century has cited the importance of the increase in the employment of women. For example, Arthur W. Calhoun, in the third volume of *A Social History of the American Family,* published in 1919, wrote that "the fact of woman's access to industry must be a prime factor in opening to her the possibility of separation from husband." Willard Waller commented in his 1938 text on the family that the employment of wives often created an opposition of interests in the family, in contrast to the interdependence found in preindustrial families. William J. Goode noted in 1963 that the possibility that a wife can support herself, even if poorly, was one of the changes that had created new alternatives to existing marriages. More recently, Carl N. Degler argued in his comprehensive history of women and the family in America that the expanding economic opportunities for women were a necessary condition for the long-term increase in divorce. Few writers believe that women's employment is a direct cause of marital dissolution; rather, they suggest that the widening opportunities for woman allow couples to separate who are unhappy with their marriages for other reasons.[43]

The employment of a wife could conceivably have quite different effects on marital stability. The earnings she brings home could ease her family's financial burden and reduce the tensions of economic hardship, thereby reducing the likelihood of marital dissolution. Or her work might bring her increased personal satisfaction, which would, in turn, improve her relationship with her husband. To sort out these effects, a number of researchers have examined data from studies of married women who were followed during the 1970s. Most of these analyses show that, other things being equal, married women who worked outside the home were more likely to divorce or separate in the next few years—although it remains unclear whether it is the fact of working outside the home, the number of hours worked, or the amount of income earned that matters.[44] The studies also showed that many other characteristics of the wife and her husband affected the probability of marital breakup, including age at marriage and whether the husband is stably employed.[45] The connection between wives' work and divorce also could operate in the other direction: one study of married women in the 1970s found evidence that, well before a divorce, those who would subsequently divorce increased the amount of time they worked outside the home. The authors suggest that some married women may work more hours in anticipation of a divorce.[46] In either case, it appears that on balance work outside the home reduces a woman's dependence on her husband and makes it easier for a couple to end an unhappy marriage.

Most of these studies investigated the relationship of employment to marriage and divorce at the individual level. More pertinent is whether an analogous relationship held at the societal level during the postwar period. From the research reviewed in this chapter, it is possible to make three statements: (1) a married woman may be more likely to divorce if she is in the labor force; (2) the labor force participation rate for younger married women rose sharply after 1960; and (3) younger married women are in general more likely to divorce than are older married women. These statements, I believe, build a plausible case that the sharp increase in young married women's participation in the labor force in the 1960s and 1970s contributed to the rise in divorce. The evidence remains circumstantial; but it seems to me that it is stronger and more suggestive than that linking any other concurrent trend with the rise in divorce.

There are, however, alternative explanations for the parallel rise in young women's rate of employment, average age at marriage, and probability of divorce. Easterlin argues that the movement of wives into the labor force and the trends in marriage and divorce after 1960 were both determined by a more fundamental trend—a decline in the income of young men relative to the income of their parents while they were growing up. As I have said, Easterlin explained the trends of the 1950s in terms of the relatively favorable income position of the young men of the small cohorts born in the 1920s and 1930s. One result of this postwar development, however, was that the next generation—the cohorts born during the late 1940s and 1950s—was very large. Easterlin contends that because the members of the baby boom cohorts grew up during a time of relative affluence, they acquired a high standard of living. Unfortunately, when the large numbers of young men of the baby boom came of age in the 1960s and 1970s, they found increased competition for good jobs. Many may have had to settle for employment that offered less than they had hoped.

The situation of the cohort of the late 1940s and 1950s, then, was the opposite of that of the cohorts of the 1920s and 1930s, according to Easterlin: the younger cohorts had high expectations as they entered a tight labor market; the older cohorts had modest expectations as they entered a more favorable market. This relative decline in opportunity, he argues, caused the young men and women of the baby boom to marry at a later age, on the average, than did their parents' generation. The relatively unfavorable income position of the young men, combined with their taste for material goods, meant that many young married couples postponed having children. Instead, many of the young wives went to work to supplement the family's income. In addition, he argues, increased marital conflict fueled by the tight economic situation led to the sharp increase in divorce. Easterlin doesn't rule out the possibility that the increased employment of young married women had an independent effect on marital dissolution, but he does suggest that both the increasing employment of wives and the increase in dissolution resulted ultimately from the deteriorating income position of young men.[47] Easterlin's explanation has the virtue of theoretical simplicity: he proposes the same model to account for the very different trends of the 1950s, the 1960s and 1970s, and the 1980s and beyond. But Easterlin's model doesn't explain why, as Figure 2-1 shows, birth and marriage rates declined for somewhat older women—those in their early-to-mid-thirties—as well in the 1960s and 1970s.[48] Most of these women were born before the baby boom; yet their behavior changed as well. The parallel movement of birth and marriage rates for all age groups suggests that a period effect—something in the air—affected all cohorts.[49]

Aside from young women's employment and young men's economic prospects, another development might have affected marriage and divorce since 1960: the introduction and widespread use of better methods of contraception—notably the birth control pill, the intrauterine device, and surgical sterilization—and the greater availability of abortion. In 1960, according to surveys conducted by Norman B. Ryder and Charles F. Westoff, less than one-tenth of all couples who weren't trying to have a child were using the pill, the IUD, or sterilization; by 1970 the proportion was one-half; by 1975 it was three-fourths.[50] Yet scholars are still debating the extent to which the increased availability of better methods of birth control brought about the decline in fertility since

1960. At issue is whether fertility fell primarily because of a change in people's motivation to use birth control or primarily because of improvements in the methods available. On the one hand, Ryder and Westoff claim that much of the decline occurred simply because more effective contraceptive methods were available. On the other hand, researchers such as Judith Blake and Prithwis Das Gupta maintain that the more significant change was in people's intentions: young couples desired fewer children in the 1960s and 1970s than did their counterparts in the 1950s, as shown by public opinion surveys, and therefore they were more highly motivated to practice contraception.[51] Those who believe that changes in motivation are more important than changes in birth control technology note, for example, that the birth rate was low during the depression, when many couples wanted to postpone having children because of economic hardship, even though modern methods of contraception were lacking.[52]

It is even less clear how much of the post-1960 rise in age at marriage and in divorce can be attributed to the improvement in contraceptive technology and the availability of abortion. One might expect that greater control over childbearing would make it easier for married women to work outside the home, and I have shown that the increase in young married women's employment, in turn, has probably contributed to the increase in divorce. Similarly, many unmarried women may have avoided unwanted pregnancies because of the better birth control methods, thus preventing some early marriages, which have a higher probability of divorce, and possibly contributing to the rising age at marriage. Yet here again it may be that the introduction of better technology is of secondary importance compared to changes in young people's motivation to avoid or postpone having children. Some studies suggest that reduced childbearing was more a consequence than a cause of the long-term increase in young women's employment.[53] Although it is possible that improved birth control technology and easier access to abortion have had a significant, independent influence on age at marriage and on divorce, this influence has not yet been demonstrated convincingly.[54]

Like the explanations of the trends of the 1950s, all of these hypotheses about the trends in marriage, divorce, and childbearing in the 1960s

and 1970s can be considered as either period or cohort explanations.
Partisans of period explanations argue that some of the long-term
changes characterizing advanced industrial societies accelerated in the
United States after 1960, producing a rise in the age at marriage, a large
increase in divorce, and a sharp drop in childbearing. They emphasize
the importance of the increased participation in the labor force among
young married women, the development and dissemination of better
contraceptive technology, or the liberalization of attitudes toward divorce. Those who subscribe to this view tend to see the depression and
the war as temporary interruptions, disturbances whose effects faded
after the 1950s. On the other hand, scholars such as Easterlin who
propose cohort explanations maintain that the low birth rates during
the depression set in motion swings in cohort size that will, in turn,
produce in each successive generation swings in rates of marriage,
divorce, and childbearing.

Why, then, were couples more likely to divorce in 1980 than in 1960,
and why were they likely to have married at a later age? To some extent,
the changes after 1960 represent a movement back to more typical
patterns of marrying and divorcing. Yet the very large increase in
divorce during the 1960s and 1970s and the continuing increase in age
at marriage need to be accounted for. By the 1970s, Americans were
more tolerant of single and divorced persons, and this shift may have
encouraged more people to delay marriage or to divorce. Later marriage
and more divorce may in turn have stimulated a further liberalization
of attitudes, creating a kind of attitude-behavior feedback loop. But as
I have argued, it is doubtful that attitudinal change was a major force
in initiating the trends in the 1960s.

I think the increased labor force participation of young married
women ultimately will be seen as the most important stimulus to the
initial rise in age at marriage and in divorce after 1960. I have argued
in this chapter that this rising participation accounted for at least part
of the change, but it is impossible as yet to say precisely how large or
small a part. It may be, as Easterlin suggests, that the less favorable
income position of young men accounted for another part, and improved contraception may also have contributed. It is not possible to
state definitively which of the effects discussed above was more import-

ant; but together they take us a long way toward accounting for the
trends in marital formation and dissolution in the 1960s and 1970s.

## The 1980s

After peaking in the late 1950s, the birth rate began to decline. In the
1980s, as a result, the relative size of the cohorts entering adulthood
began to decline. If a cyclical, cohort-size model such as Easterlin's were
driving young adults' behavior, then a reversal of the trends in marriage
and childbearing of the 1960s and 1970s should have started.[55] Young
adults should have begun to marry earlier and to have children faster,
and the flow of married women into the labor force should have slowed.
But that's not what happened. Age at marriage kept rising throughout
the decade, reaching a twentieth-century high for women (see Figure
1-1). The increase in married women's labor force participation—the
only constant in a sea of change since World War II—continued its
relentless march (see Figure 2-4). It is true that the birth rate rose
somewhat. But the rise occurred in births to the wrong women. There
was no increase among women in their twenties, the young adults who
supposedly should have benefited from the smaller cohort size. Instead,
the rise occurred almost entirely to women in their thirties and forties.
It was catch-up fertility—an increase among the older women from
larger cohorts who had postponed childbearing while in their twenties
and were trying to make up for lost time.

In sum, there was no return to younger marriage and childbearing
in the 1980s. A partisan of cohort-based explanations might argue that
the real test of the cyclical model won't occur until the 1990s. The birth
rate was still fairly high, although declining, throughout much of the
1960s; it didn't bottom out until the 1970s. So the smallest cohorts have
just begun to reach adulthood. Still, even if the cohort-size model wasn't
knocked out by the 1980s, it's certainly on the ropes.

The fundamental weakness of the cohort-size model was its assumption that employed wives aren't very committed to working outside the
home—that a wife's work is still seen as secondary to her husband's
work, as a supplement to his earnings that can be forgone if he gets a
nice raise. This is a reasonable description of what most people believed

in the 1950s and 1960s. But about 1970, popular opinion began to shift to a much more positive view of married women's employment. Figure 2-5 assembles data on the work attitudes of women of childbearing age, based on national surveys conducted during the 1970s and 1980s. From the vantage point of the 1990s, it is startling to find that in 1970, just two decades ago, four out of five ever-married women under 45 agreed that "it is much better for everyone involved if the man is the achiever outside the home and the woman takes care of the home and the family." More than two-thirds agreed that "a preschool child is likely to suffer if his or her mother works." Only half agreed with the

*Figure 2-5.* Attitudes toward work and family, for ever-married women less than age 45, 1970, 1977, 1985, and 1989 (percentage agreeing among all who gave an opinion). A: "It is much better for everyone involved if the man is the achiever outside the home and the woman takes care of the home and family." B: "A preschool child is likely to suffer if his or her mother works." C: "A working mother can establish just as warm a relationship with her children as a mother who does not work." Sources: for 1970, National Fertility Survey; for 1977, 1985, and 1989, National Opinion Research Center, General Social Surveys.

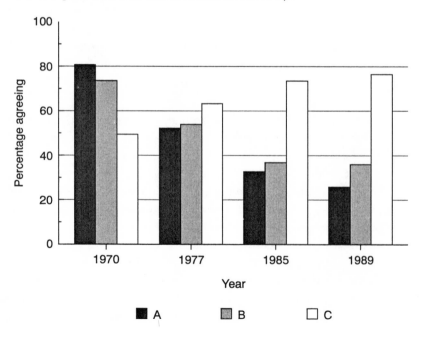

statement that "a working mother can establish just as warm and secure a relationship with her children as a mother who does not work." Clearly, as recently as 1970, American women were quite traditional in their attitudes toward women's proper work role. These traditional attitudes didn't stop many of them from working, but something other than a belief in the desirability of working outside the home must have influenced their decisions to work.

During the 1970s and 1980s, as Figure 2-5 shows, a complete reversal of opinion occurred. By 1989, only 26 percent of ever-married women under 45 agreed that it is better for everyone if the wife stays home—the mirror image of the responses in 1970. Just 36 percent agreed that preschool children suffer if their mothers work. Fully 77 percent agreed that a working mother can establish just as warm and secure a relationship with her children. This dramatic change was well underway by the late 1970s. At the start of this period, most women viewed employment as a potential danger to the family; at the end most thought it benign. The attitudes of men toward women's employment also became less traditional in the 1970s and 1980s. In several surveys done between 1972 and 1989, national samples of adult men and women were asked, "Do you approve of a married woman earning money in business or industry if she has a husband capable of supporting her?" In 1972, 63 percent of men approved; in 1989 79 percent approved.[56] (The comparable figures for women were 68 percent in 1972 and 79 percent in 1989.)

It appears that before 1970 changes in attitudes were not nearly as rapid. Figure 2-6 displays the responses of men and women over the past fifty years to survey questions about whether they would vote for a woman for president. Although this question takes us a bit far afield from female labor force participation, it is one of the few questions about women's roles that has been asked regularly for the past several decades in national surveys. There are some problems in comparing the responses over time—the exact wording of the question has varied, as have the sampling techniques of the surveys—but the general trend is probably reliable. The percentage of American women who said they would vote for a woman for president increased gradually from the late 1930s to the late 1960s and then increased at a much faster rate through

*Figure 2-6.* Percentage who would vote for a woman for President, by sex, 1937–1989. Sources: for 1937–1969, George H. Gallup, *The Gallup Poll: Public Opinion 1935–1971*, vols. 1–3 (New York: Random House, 1972); for 1972–1989, National Opinion Research Center, General Social Surveys.


the mid-1970s. The proportion of men willing to vote for a woman increased fairly steadily throughout the fifty-year period; but even so, the 1970s were a time of particularly rapid change. The increases for both women and men continued until the mid-1980s, at which point nearly nine out of ten women and men said they would vote for a woman. If the pattern of change shown here is representative of sex-role attitudes in general, it would suggest that attitudes became more liberal rather slowly and gradually before the late 1960s. Throughout the first twenty years of the postwar period, then, the rising rates of female participation in the labor force coexisted with widespread traditional beliefs about women's roles.

It seems that changes in attitudes about women's roles could not have been a major force behind the trends in female labor force participation, marriage, divorce, and childbearing prior to 1970. Most of the young

married women who entered the labor force in the 1960s apparently
went to work because they felt that they needed the money or that the
psychic benefits outweighed the costs to their families. Yet the dramatic
changes in attitudes since the late 1960s suggest that the greater acceptance of employment for married women may now play an independent
role. It is possible, of course, that attitudes about women's roles could
change in the near future, but I think a sharp reversal is unlikely. The
spread of nontraditional attitudes will mean that more young married
women will wish to remain at work; thus any improvements in young
men's economic situation will have less of an effect on trends in marriage, divorce, and childbearing.

Even if attitudinal change is discounted, young women's labor force
participation rates probably will remain high. When the OPEC cartel
caused the first oil price shock in 1973, the postwar surge in wages came
crashing to a halt. Since then, family income (adjusted for inflation)
has remained stagnant. The economist Frank Levy tells this story best
in a book about the American income distribution since the war.[57] Levy
notes that the gap between the incomes of younger male workers and
older male workers widened considerably during the 1970s and 1980s.
For example, the income gap between 30-year-old and 50-year-old men
widened from 19 percent in 1975 to 36 percent in 1984. In addition, as
Levy notes, housing prices in the 1970s rose much more rapidly than
the prices of other goods—or than wages. For the first time since the
war, young men weren't living better than their fathers had at their age.
For a generation that was raised in the 1950s and 1960s and had high
expectations for the future, the stagnation in the 1970s and 1980s and
the rise in housing prices led to profound disappointment. The main
way that young married couples coped was to have both spouses work
outside the home. By the mid-1980s a majority of families in the upper
half of the income distribution had working wives.[58] A second income
became increasingly necessary to stay in the middle class.

It is possible, of course, that the economy will rebound, wages will
increase, and single-earner families will be better able to sustain a
middle class standard of living. But a number of observers believe that
the stagnation in incomes results from the globalization of the economy—the movement overseas of factories and assembly lines and the

jobs that go with them. According to this argument, as semi-skilled factory jobs have declined, American workers have shifted to the service sector, where output per worker cannot grow as fast. The result is a two-tiered economy, with high-paying professional jobs and low-paying service jobs.[59]

Levy reports that his examination of census data uncovered little evidence of a trend toward a two-tiered economy. Rather, what happened in the 1970s and early 1980s, he argues, was a "quiet depression" caused by a temporary imbalance of supply (a large cohort of young adults) and demand (a poorly performing economy). Its roots "have less to do with the changing industrial structure than with a bad period in our economic life."[60] I think Levy is correct that statistical evidence doesn't support alarmist warnings that we are turning into a nation of either hamburger flippers or investment bankers. His reminder that the extremely rapid income growth of the 1950s and 1960s was unusual resonates with the unusual family patterns of the 1950s and early 1960s. Nevertheless, as the 1990s begin, the "bad period" is still with us. "Bad times are not forever," states the upbeat last sentence of Levy's book; but this one is nearing its twentieth anniversary. As Levy himself has noted in recent presentations, income inequality worsened throughout the 1980s, despite the recovery from the Reagan recession.[61] The suspicion grows that perhaps a structural shift indeed has occurred, that too many factories indeed have moved to Mexico, Korea, or Taiwan, and that the position of American workers in the international division of labor makes it difficult for the less well-educated to find a job that can support a family. If so, it is less likely than ever that married women will leave the labor force in large numbers.

## The General and the Particular

Overall, the trends in marriage, divorce, and childbearing since World War II appear to have been the result of a general, long-term historical process, on the one hand, and two specific historical events, on the other hand. The long-term process is the development of advanced industrial societies, one characteristic of which has been an increase over time in the proportion of married women who work outside the home. In the years between World War II and the oil price shock of 1973, this trend accelerated in the United States because of increases in the demand for female workers in the service sector, rising real wages of employed women, and better control over fertility. Since 1973, stagnant wages of male workers and sweeping changes in attitudes about the employment of women have played an important role. The great increase in female employment has altered, perhaps permanently, men's and women's roles in the family. Employment has made many married women less dependent on their husbands for support, and this development, in turn, may have increased the likelihood that unhappy couples will resort to divorce. Greater employment opportunities may have induced many single women to wait longer before marrying. At the same time, improved contraception—another postwar development—may have influenced the trends by allowing couples to control the timing of childbearing, thus reducing unwanted births and helping women organize their work lives. Together, these society-wide changes in women's work lives and reproductive lives have promoted the acceleration of the long-term rise in divorce and the long-term fall in fertility that has characterized the United States since the mid-nineteenth century.

The specific historical events that interrupted these long-term patterns were the Great Depression and World War II. The disruption of family life and childbearing in the 1930s and the war years seems to have brought about, paradoxically, greater stability of family life and an increase in childbearing in the 1950s. This occurred, in part, through the social-psychological mechanism of instilling in the men and women born in the 1920s and 1930s a greater sense of the value of family life and childrearing and lowered expectations of material comfort. A satisfying family life became a more scarce resource during the depression and the war and, like most scarce resources, its value increased correspondingly. In addition, the depression influenced the trends of the 1950s by reducing the size of the cohorts of the 1920s and 1930s. As a result of their small numbers, they were better able to take advantage of the opportunities offered by the postwar economic prosperity, and they were more likely to have the resources necessary to start or to enlarge their families.

It is unlikely that the legacy of the depression and the war will continue to influence marriage, divorce, and childbearing in the 1990s and the early twenty-first century. Some believe that the depression set in motion long swings in fertility, marriage, and divorce that will continue indefinitely. A close examination of the postwar trends, however, shows that most of the changes seem to have occurred among every group at the same time—suggesting that current conditions, not historical events, were the prime moving force. It is true that in the 1950s women and men in their early-to-mid-twenties changed their marriage and childbearing patterns even more than did slightly older cohorts. I find it plausible that the values of people who grew up during the hard times of the 1930s were determined in large part by their childhood and adolescent experiences. Consequently, Easterlin can argue that some of the young couples in the 1950s brought to their marriages an expectation of a modest standard of living that was unlikely to change, and Elder can argue that some also brought a strong preference for marriage and childbearing.

Yet it does not follow that growing up after 1950 will determine adult preferences to the same extent. The young couples who married in the 1980s and are marrying in the 1990s did not as children face a momentous, life-altering experience like the depression. Despite their decreasing cohort size, they should be more likely as adults to modify their preferences for material goods, children, employment, and so forth as current circumstances change. And circumstances seem to me to be changing in such a way as to encourage the continued entry of women into the labor force—witness the sharp changes in sex-role attitudes displayed in Figure 2-5 and the lack of growth in family income. Thus, I suspect that the cycles predicted by Easterlin will be similar to the damped oscillations of a child's swing: unless there is a further push from another depression or another world war, the swings will become progressively smaller and eventually fade altogether.

The process of change in postwar family life may be similar to the process of change in family life during the early years of industrialization. In his study of mid-nineteenth-century Hamilton, an industrializing city in what is now Ontario, Michael B. Katz found evidence that between 1851 and 1871 teenage youths became more dependent on their parents and that the foundation was laid for the stage of prolonged dependency we now call adolescence. In this and other ways, he argued, family ties and commitments grew stronger over time. Katz ascribed these changes to industrialization in general and to the depression of the late 1850s in particular: "Any adequate explanation of this developmental process," he wrote, "must combine the interaction of long-term processes, such as modernization, with short-term crises, like depressions, which may accelerate or retard their pace. Only a theory which accommodates both the general and the particular can encompass adequately the kind of data presented here."[62] The same might be said of the explanations of trends in marriage, divorce, and childbearing since World War II.

# 3

# Consequences

What does it mean for people's lives and for the institution of the family when about one out of six young women is likely to be still unmarried at age thirty, when nearly half of all adults will live with a partner before marrying, when about one out of two recent marriages will end in divorce, when about one-third of all young adults can expect to find themselves eventually in a remarriage following a divorce?[1] In this chapter I examine the significance of these trends for the lives of individual adults and children and for the family patterns of American society. First, I look at the ways in which the trends in marriage, divorce, and remarriage have affected patterns of family life in our society as a whole. I examine the changes in the typical life course of Americans, in the composition of households and families, and in the role of marriage. Second, I consider the effects of divorce and remarriage on the well-being of individual adults and children.

## Lifetime Histories

Consider the lifetime marriage and divorce histories for four birth cohorts of women: those born in 1908 to 1912, 1928 to 1932, 1948 to 1950, and 1970. These four cohorts are roughly representative of four successive generations of Americans—those born early in the century, their daughters born around the time of the Great Depression, their granddaughters born during the first years of the postwar baby boom, and their great-granddaughters, the children of the baby boomers. Figure 3-1 shows the cumulative percentage experiencing each of four events: a first marriage, a divorce, a remarriage after a divorce, and a second divorce. For the first three cohorts, the estimates of marriage, first divorce, and remarriage are from "marital status life tables" produced by Robert Schoen and his colleagues using historical data; the

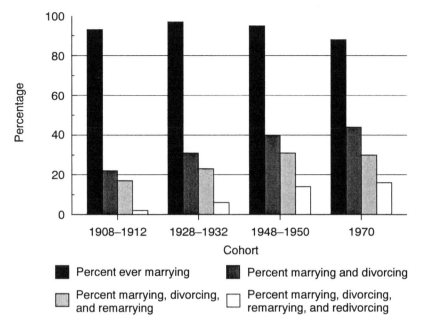

*Figure 3-1.* Percentage ever marrying, divorcing, remarrying, and redivorcing for four birth cohorts of women, 1908–1912, 1928–1932, 1948–1950, and 1970. Sources: See notes 2, 3, and 4.

estimates of second divorce were produced by the Bureau of the Census.[2] The women in the fourth cohort, born in 1970, are just now beginning to marry. Figure 3-1 shows what their lifetime experiences would be if they were to marry and divorce at the rates prevailing in 1990. So the fourth set of bars is merely a projection of the lifetime patterns implied by current rates of marriage and divorce.[3]

First of all, almost everyone in the first three cohorts has married—93 percent of the oldest cohort according to Schoen, 97 percent of the Depression cohort, and a projected 95 percent of the early baby boom cohort. For the youngest cohort, the proportion ever-married may fall a percentage point or two below the 90 percent mark. There are much greater differences among the cohorts in the percentages who marry *and* divorce: only 22 percent of the women born in 1908 to 1912 have been married and divorced, but this rises to an estimated 31 percent for the women born during the depression, 40 percent for the early baby boom women, and 44 percent among the youngest women.[4] The differences continue in the percentages that ever marry, divorce, *and* remarry: 17 percent for the 1908 to 1912 cohort, an estimated 23 percent for the 1928 to 1932 cohort, 31 percent for the 1948 to 1950 cohort, and 30 percent for the 1970 cohort. Just two percent of the oldest women experienced a second divorce, whereas 16 percent of the youngest women are projected to do so.

Figure 3-1 demonstrates the extent to which divorce and remarriage have changed from relatively rare experiences to much more common experiences during the twentieth century. If the experiences of the 1908 to 1912 cohort are representative of women born early in the century, then perhaps two in ten of the elderly women now alive were ever divorced, and almost none were divorced more than once. But for young adult women today, at least four in ten are likely to divorce; three in ten are likely to remarry following a divorce, and one in six is likely to divorce twice, if current rates continue. For the generations in between—those who were born around the time of the depression or in the early baby boom years—the lifetime levels of divorce and remarriage are also in between.

The typical ages at divorce and at remarriage also declined between the 1908 to 1912 cohort and the 1948 to 1950 cohort, according to the estimates of Schoen and his colleagues, and will probably rise somewhat in the youngest cohort.[5] These changes in timing have been less impressive, however, than the changes in the volume of divorces and remarriages from one generation to the next. During the twentieth century, and especially during the postwar years, the most notable change in patterns of marital formation and dissolution is that divorce and remarriage increasingly have become normal events in the course of a person's life.

## Households and Families

The great increases in lifetime levels of divorce and remarriage have, in turn, altered the composition of families and households. At any given time, there are many more families being maintained by a separated or divorced person than was the case before World War II or even just a generation ago. In 1990 there were 4.8 million separated or divorced mothers heading families that included children under eighteen, more than double the number in 1970.[6] Moreover, in 1985 there were 4.5 million husband-wife households that included at least one stepchild under the age of 18.[7]

Other changes also have affected the composition of households. Perhaps the most important one has been the growing likelihood that unmarried individuals will choose to maintain their own households rather than live with kin. It used to be common for a woman to move back to her parents' home after she separated from her husband, but today separated and divorced women are much more likely to set up their own households. Never-married young adults, whose numbers have been increasing, are less likely to remain at home until they marry than they were a generation or two ago.[8] Similarly, more older widowed people are living by themselves rather than moving in with their children.[9] It may be that the preferences of unmarried adults concerning living arrangements have changed. I suspect, however, that most unmarried adults always have preferred to live independently, only today they are more likely to have the financial resources to do so. In any case, the growth of households that do not contain a married couple has far outstripped the growth of husband-wife households. Between 1970 and 1990, for example, the total number of households grew by 30 million, but the number of households with a married couple grew by only 8 million.[10]

These statistics on households do have some limitations as indicators of trends in family life. People move from one household to another more frequently than in the past;[11] most of the young single adults now maintaining households, for instance, eventually will marry—and many will divorce and then marry again. The statistics on household composition give us a snapshot of the living arrangements of Americans, and this picture is valuable to policy-makers and to providers of goods and services. Yet families are increasingly extending across the boundaries of households, so that statistics about households are becoming less useful as a guide to the situation of families. Many separated, divorced, and remarried parents, for example, retain close ties to children living elsewhere, and many low-income single parents have strong family networks that extend across several households.

Nevertheless, these statistics do show us that a smaller proportion of families and households contains a husband and wife than was the case ten or twenty years ago. And the proportion of husband-wife families in which one or both partners are remarried following a divorce has increased. Families headed by a couple in their first marriage, of course, have long been the dominant family form—both numerically and normatively—in American life. But the recent changes imply that although they are still numerically dominant (albeit less so), they must share their dominant position with two other increasingly common family forms: the single-parent family and the family of remarriage. If the estimates presented in Figure 3-1 prove at all accurate, one can no longer speak of families formed by divorce and remarriage as unusual. Indeed, barring unforeseen reversals in the trends, a majority of all the children alive today will probably witness the disruption of either their parents' marriage or their own marriage by divorce. At any one time, then, the composition of families is much more diverse than was the case in the 1950s.

Still, family life continues to center around marriage for most Americans. Most cohabiting couples, as noted in Chapter 1, either marry or end their relationships within two or three years. Most people eventually marry, and most divorced people remarry—although a majority cohabit with a partner first. As others have argued, the increases in cohabitation, later marriage, and divorce don't mean that marriage is on the way out.[12] During every period of rapid increase in divorce in the United States, concerned individuals have warned of the coming demise of the family; such alarmist sentiments have always proved to be unfounded, and the warnings expressed in the 1960s and 1970s were no exception. By the beginning of the 1980s most commentators had decided that the latest reports of the imminent death of the family had been greatly exaggerated.

Having acknowledged the persistence and continuity of family life, however, I must also acknowledge that much has changed, some of it for the worse. Life in a single-parent family or a family formed by a remarriage has its unique and sometimes problematic aspects. Many more people must manage the difficult transition from being married to being divorced—a transition that seems to be no less painful merely because it is more common. And many more people must blend themselves, their children, their new spouse, and their new spouses' children into families formed by remarriages, which can prove to be a complex and difficult task.

Even first marriages have been altered by such developments as the growth of cohabitation, the changing roles of women, declining fertility, and more frequent recourse to divorce. In the 1950s Talcott Parsons argued that although some of its traditional functions were declining, the nuclear family centered on marriage was coming to specialize in two remaining functions: providing emotional support to adults and socializing young children.[13] The post-1960 changes may have allowed more people to fulfill these needs outside of marriage. Judith Blake, for instance, maintains that with more people living out of wedlock, having children out of wedlock, and voluntarily ending the state of wedlock, the line between being married and being unmarried has become increasingly blurred.[14] I think Blake may have overstated the lack of a distinctive role for marriage—as I argued in Chapter 1, cohabitation seems to be less an alternative to marriage than a precursor—but it seems to be true that the functions of marriage increasingly can be fulfilled in other ways.

Thus many of the traditional reasons why people got married and stayed married are less compelling today. Sexual relations are practiced and accepted outside of marriage to an unprecedented degree. The greater economic independence of women means that marriage is less necessary as an economic partnership, as a common enterprise that creates a joint product neither partner could produce alone. And as the success of the economic enterprise becomes less crucial to husbands and wives, their personal satisfaction with their marriage becomes relatively more important. Consequently, husbands and wives are more likely today than in the past to evaluate their marriage primarily according to how well it satisfies their individual emotional needs. If their evaluation on these terms is unfavorable, they are likely to turn to divorce and then, perhaps, to another marriage.

On a societal level, therefore, patterns of marriage and family life are very different from what they were just a few decades ago. The statistics I have presented suggest that among the most significant differences are the increasing levels of divorce and remarriage and the associated rise in the number of single-parent families and families formed by remarriage. When we shift our view from society to individuals, we find, not surprisingly, that the daily lives of adults and children in these post-divorce families differ in important ways from the typical experiences of people in families of first marriages.

## Family Life after Divorce

Although social scientists have long been concerned about divorce, they produced little empirical research about its consequences until the 1970s. Since then, they have begun to establish a body of knowledge about its effects on adults and children. On the one hand, recent studies lend qualified support to the view that divorce can be beneficial in the long run for some of those involved. For instance, researchers have produced findings in support of the oft-stated claim that children function better in a single-parent family than in a conflict-ridden nuclear family.[15] On the other hand, the studies also show that divorce is a traumatic process that can cause serious short-term psychological distress. There is evidence that for some adults and children, the harmful effects may be longer lasting.

Developmental psychologists P. Lindsay Chase-Lansdale and E. Mavis Hetherington suggest that the first two years following the breakup of a marriage constitute a "crisis period."[16] During this difficult time adults and children typically face intense emotional upset, continuing family conflict, and adjustments to new living arrangements. When children are involved—as they are in more than half of all divorces—they usually live with their mothers, whose daily routine is often disrupted during the first year after divorce. Hetherington followed for six years a group of middle-class families who had recently divorced and a comparison group of two-parent families. All of the families initially had preschool-aged children. She reported the predominance just after the divorce of a "chaotic lifestyle," as one participant called it, which seemed to persist throughout the first year after divorce and then improve in the second year. Single mothers and their children in the divorced families were more likely to eat pickup meals at irregular times, the children's bedtimes were erratic, the children were more likely to arrive at school late, and so forth.[17]

Saddled with sole or primary responsibility for supporting themselves and their children, single mothers frequently have too little time and too few resources to manage effectively. Robert S. Weiss, after several years of observing single parents, identified three common sources of strain. One is responsibility overload: single parents must make all the decisions and provide for all the needs of their families, a responsibility that at times can be overwhelming. Another is task overload: many single parents simply have too much to do, with working, housekeeping, and parenting; consequently, there is no slack time to meet unexpected demands. A third is emotional overload: single parents are always on call to give emotional support to their children, whether or not their own emotional resources are temporarily depleted.[18]

Moreover, divorced and separated women who are raising children often find that their economic position has deteriorated. Many of those who were not employed in the years preceding their separation have difficulty reentering the job market. Others who were employed find that their wages are too low to support a family. In theory, divorced fathers should continue to help support their children, but in practice only a minority do so adequately. Some avoid a legal agreement altogether: in a 1989 Bureau of the Census survey, 19 percent of all divorced and separated women living with children under 21 reported that they wanted child support but couldn't obtain an award for reasons such as the inability to find their ex-husbands. Even among divorced and separated women who were supposed to receive child support payments, 22 percent reported receiving nothing in 1989. And among those who were fortunate enough to receive any payments in 1989, the average amount received was just $3,322 for the divorced and $3,060 for the separated.[19]

As a result of their limited earning power and of the low level of child support, single mothers and their children often experience a sharp decline in their standard of living after a separation. In the Panel Study of Income Dynamics (PSID), a national study of families who were interviewed annually beginning in 1968, separated and divorced women suffered an average drop of about 30 percent in their standard of living in the year following a marital break-up. Men, in contrast, experienced a rise of 10 to 15 percent because they no longer fully supported their wives and children.[20] Middle-class homemakers suffered the largest average declines. They had agreed to take care of the home and the children full time in return for their husbands' provision of all financial support. When that bargain broke down, they became dependent on meager child support payments and whatever low-paying jobs their neglected labor market skills could command. Among women in the PSID who had above-average family incomes just prior to the separation, 31 percent saw their standard of living in the year after the separation plunge by more than half.[21]

Many single parents, particularly those with low incomes, receive assistance from a network of kin, but the resources of these networks usually are limited and spread thin. Economic pressure on the mother means that she has less time for child care and for her personal life. Harried and overburdened, some single mothers fail to provide the attention and care children need, especially during the first year or two after the separation.

To be sure, life in a single-parent family, despite economic pressures, also has its rewards, foremost the relief from marital conflict. In addition, single parents may gain increased self-esteem from their ability to manage the demands of work life and family life by themselves. They may enjoy their independence and their close relationships to their children.[22] Some writers argue that women are particularly likely to develop an increased sense of self-worth from the independence and greater control over their life they achieve after divorce.[23]

Psychologically, the period following the separation is likely to be very stressful for both spouses, regardless of who initiated the break-up. Both spouses commonly retain ambivalent feelings toward their partners even if they were relieved to have ended an unhappy marriage. For example, Weiss studied adults who came to a series of eight-week discussion and counseling sessions he organized in Boston for persons separated less than one year. Most reported a persistent feeling of attachment to their spouse, a sense of bonding that continued for several months whether the participant had initiated the separation or not. Thus many of the separated adults who attended Weiss's seminars felt an intermittent longing for their husbands or wives and an accompanying anxiety that Weiss labeled "separation distress." Only after the first year of separation did this attachment fade.[24]

Overall, then, the first year after divorce or separation is often a time when the separated spouses experience ambivalence about the separation, increased anxiety, occasional depression, and personal disorganization—even if they were the ones who chose to end their marriages. And it is a time when the income of mothers with custody of their children often drops sharply. Within a year, however, most separated adults have begun the process of reorganizing their lives, although it may take a few years more to establish a stable identity and a new life situation.[25]

Children too experience an initial period of intense emotional upset after their parents separate. Judith S. Wallerstein and Joan B. Kelly studied 131 children from 60 recently separated families who sought the services of a counseling center in Marin County, California. They met with the children at the time of the divorce action and then again eighteen months, five years, and ten years later. At first, according to their study, almost all the children were profoundly upset. Their reactions varied according to age. Preschool children tended to be frightened and bewildered by the separation and to blame themselves for what had occurred; older children often expressed great anger. Adolescents were better able to comprehend the reasons for the divorce, but they often were deeply worried about the effects of the separation on their own future.[26]

A number of studies suggest that the short-term adjustment to divorce is different for boys than for girls. Boys in conflict-ridden families—whether or not a separation has occurred—show more aggressive and antisocial behavior, whereas girls are less prone to do so.[27] Hetherington and others have identified "coercive cycles" between mothers and their preschool sons that can occur soon after a divorce: mothers, who may be overburdened, angry, and depressed, respond irritably to the whining and difficult behavior of their distressed sons, only to aggravate the very behavior they try to quell.[28] Girls appear to adjust to a separation more rapidly and to exhibit more "good" behavior. But there is some evidence that they internalize their distress more and, despite outward adjustment, may suffer from depression or lowered self-esteem.[29]

Less is known about long-term adjustment to divorce. Hetherington found marked improvement in the relations between many of the parents and their preschool children between the first and second year after the divorce. One-half of the mothers and one-fourth of the fathers reported that by two years after the divorce their relationships with their children had improved over the tension-filled last days of their marriages.[30] The majority of the children had resumed normal development. But in one type of family, problems tended to linger: six years after the divorce, when the children in Hetherington's study were ten, mothers who had not remarried reported more loneliness and depression and a lower sense of control over the course of their lives. Their relationships with their sons were more likely to include the ineffective parenting and coercive cycles found between mothers and sons during the crisis period. In contrast, relationships between non-remarried mothers and their daughters were similar to mother-daughter relationships in families in which no divorce had occurred.[31]

Wallerstein paints a very pessimistic picture of long-term adjustment. The older males, who were 19 to 29 at the ten-year follow-up, were said to be "unhappy and lonely" and to have had "few, if any, lasting relationships with young women." Many of the older girls, she and her co-author Sandra Blakeslee stated, appeared well adjusted at first but encountered problems years later. At the ten-year mark, most of the 19-to-23-year-old women were said to be overcome by fear and anxiety at the prospect of making an emotional commitment to a man.[32] But although Wallerstein's clinical study contains many insights, the prevalence of long-term problems in the general population of divorced children almost certainly is lower than she reports for her sample. Families were referred to her clinic for short-term therapy by lawyers, clergy, and occasionally court authorities. Many of the parents had prior mental health problems.[33] In addition, Wallerstein didn't compare her children with a control group of children in families that were not disrupted, so it is difficult to judge how many of the problems exhibited by her subjects are common to all children, whether or not their parents have divorced. Given the nature of the study, then, it is perhaps surprising to discover that nearly half of the children survived the divorce with little or no lasting impairment. Sixty-eight percent of the younger children and somewhat less than 40 percent of the older children were said to be doing well at the ten-year follow-up.

Nevertheless, there is evidence from national surveys that growing up in a single-parent family is associated with diminished chances for a successful adult life. Using data from several national surveys of adults, Sara McLanahan and her colleagues have shown that those who report living in a single-parent family as a child are more likely subsequently to drop out of high school, marry during their teenage years, have a child before marrying, and experience the disruption of their own marriages.[34] Part of the association is due to the lower income in single-parent families, which itself increases the risk of undesirable outcomes such as dropping out of school. But McLanahan estimates that low income accounts for only about half of the story. What is behind the other half isn't clear, but it may include inadequate supervision and discipline by some single parents, the influence of the kinds of disadvantaged neighborhoods that many single parents tend to live in, or other family characteristics that make both living in a single-parent family and experiencing negative outcomes more likely.[35]

Still, most persons who grow up in a single-parent family don't drop out of high school, don't marry as teenagers, and don't have a first child before marrying. For example, McLanahan and Bumpass report that in one national survey of women age 15 to 44, 25 percent of marriages had been disrupted among those who had lived with only one natural parent at age 14, compared to about 14 percent among those who had lived with both parents, controlling for other factors. These percentages can be interpreted in two ways. On the one hand, adults from single-parent families are more likely to experience the disruption of their own marriages. On the other hand, most adults from single-parent families are still in their first marriages. So although growing up in a single-parent family increases the risk of detrimental outcomes later in life, it is not true that most adults who grew up in single-parent families will experience those outcomes.[36]

Nationally representative studies of children produce a similar pattern of findings: the negative effects of divorce are real and persistent, but only a minority experience severe negative consequences. One such study is the 1981 National Survey of Children (NSC), which included a random sample of 227 young adolescents from maritally disrupted families and a larger sample from intact, two-parent families. Paul Allison and Frank Furstenberg found that adolescents who had experienced the divorce or separation of their parents differed only modestly, on average, from those whose parents remained married on a wide variety of outcomes such as school achievement, delinquency, and psychological well-being.

The national surveys provide samples that are much more representative of the average child's experience of marital disruption than do the small-scale studies of white middle-class families that constitute the psychological literature. But the brief, structured interviews in the national surveys cannot yield the kind of in-depth information provided by the intensive, repeated testing and observation of studies such as Hetherington's. Consequently, even with the results of national surveys in hand, there are still no firm estimates of the proportion of children who experience harmful psychological effects from parental divorce. It seems unlikely to me that nearly as many will flounder in the long run as Wallerstein predicts. But taking into account what is known from recent studies, we might conclude that: (1) almost all children experience an initial period of great emotional upset following a parental separation; (2) most return to a normal developmental course within one or two years following the separation, and (3) a minority of children experience some long-term psychological problems as a result of the break-up that may persist into adulthood.

Not all children respond similarly to divorce. There are important differences among children, even within the same family, in temperament and in relations with other family members. Some children are simply more resilient to stress than others. Some manage to find safe niches that insulate them from the trauma of divorce. For example, they may have a special relationship with another adult, or they may be buffered from the conflict by one parent.[37] Furthermore, not all divorces have the same consequences for children. This latter statement might seem obvious, but until recently there wasn't enough research evidence to determine the different pathways that help or hinder children's adjustment to parental divorce.

Nevertheless, I think that two conclusions can be drawn: First, children do better when the custodial parent—usually the mother—can reestablish an orderly and supportive household routine. Hetherington refers to the benefits for children of an "authoritative" parenting style, which combines warmth and involvement with supervision and "moderately high but responsive" control.[38] When the custodial parent can keep the house in order, get the children to school and to bed on time, maintain disciplinary standards consistently but without undue harshness, and provide love and warmth, children can draw support from the parent and from the structure of their daily routine. But carrying out these childrearing tasks can be difficult for overburdened, financially strapped, emotionally upset single parents. During the crisis period, when the parent may be anxiety-ridden, harried, or depressed and the household may be disorganized, the children lose another pillar—often the last remaining pillar—of support. The custodial parent, then, can help children by functioning effectively as a parent.

Second, children do better when there is less conflict between their parents. This principle applies to intact two-parent homes as well as to families of divorce. In fact, studies show that children living with a single parent show fewer behavioral problems than do children living in homes in which two angry parents argue persistently.[39] When conflict remains after the break-up, children do better if they are shielded from the disputes. If parents can communicate, despite the conflict, and can cooperate on childrearing tasks, their children benefit. Parents who use their children as pawns or who urge their children to take sides in the battle between the mother and father often increase the child's difficulties.[40]

It is less clear whether children do better, on average, when they have a continuing relationship with both parents after the separation. The Hetherington and Wallerstein studies found that regular visits by the noncustodial parent—usually the father—helped the child greatly.[41] But other recent observational studies have not found this relationship.[42] Moreover, in the 1981 NSC, children who had regular visits with their noncustodial fathers were just as likely as those with infrequent visits to have problems in school or to engage in delinquent behavior or early sexual activity.[43] In any case, the amount of contact between children and their noncustodial fathers is shockingly low. In the NSC, half of the children from maritally disrupted homes who were living with their mothers had not seen their fathers in the last year. Just one-sixth of these children, who were then age 12 to 16, were seeing their fathers as often as once a week.[44] Much of the drop-off in contact occurred in the first two years after the disruption. Why so many fathers fade away is still unclear. Some remarry and form new families; others move away, or their ex-wife and children move away from them; still others may find that frequent visits produce too much guilt and sadness. Whatever the case, most children are deprived of a valuable continuing relationship that might help them develop and adjust.

## Family Life after Remarriage

For most divorced men and women, living as a single adult is a temporary phase in a process of decoupling and recoupling. As noted in Chapter 1, most divorced persons remarry—about two-thirds of the women and three-fourths of the men. It appears that most people who remarry cohabit with their partners first. Indeed, cohabitation after divorce has become so common that rates of union formation—cohabiting or marital—have remained roughly constant despite declines in the rate of remarriage.

In the United States and other western societies, remarriage has been the traditional answer to many of the problems faced by single parents. In the Plymouth Colony, for example, it was not unusual for one parent to die before the children reached adulthood. Most of the widows and widowers remarried within a short time, according to a study by John Demos, often within one year. The surviving parent, Demos emphasized, remarried quickly not out of any lack of respect for the deceased spouse but rather because it took two parents to meet the demands of raising a family in the harsh environment of the colony.[45] Today, despite the changes in American society, many divorced parents remarry because they need assistance in similar ways. Remarriage improves the financial situation of a divorced mother and provides another adult to share the household tasks and responsibilities. In addition, remarrying is a way to end the loneliness and isolation many divorced persons experience.

Whereas divorce often weakens the ties between children and their relatives on the side of the noncustodial parent (usually the father), remarriage creates a new set of relationships with a stepparent and his or her kin. When at least one spouse has children from a previous marriage, the family of remarriage can extend far beyond the bounds of the family of first marriage. Stepparents, stepchildren, stepsiblings, stepgrandparents, the new spouses of noncustodial parents, and other kin all may play a role in family life. This expanded set of family relationships in a remarriage can help compensate children for the loss of kin they may suffer after their parents divorce. Children whose custodial parent remarries often seem to inherit not only a stepparent but also a set of stepgrandparents and other step-kin. And since many children retain some contact with their noncustodial parent and grandparents, some children whose parents remarry may have contact with more kin than they did before their father and mother separated. But the introduction of these new relationships can also cause at least temporary problems for parents and children.

When children retain contact with their noncustodial parents, they create links between households; their visits can require communication among the divorced parents, the new stepparent, and the noncustodial parent's new spouse. In practice, most children have only infrequent contact with their noncustodial parent. Nevertheless, the great increases in divorce and remarriage have made these links across households so common that conceptions of family and kinship have been altered. To illustrate, let us consider the case in which a married couple with two children divorces and the wife retains custody of the children, as shown in panel A of Figure 3-2. If we ask the divorced mother who is in her immediate family, she certainly would include her children, but she might well exclude her ex-husband, who now lives elsewhere. If we ask her children who is in their immediate family, however, we might get a different answer. If the children still see their father regularly, they probably would include both their father and their mother as part of their family.[46] And if we ask the ex-husband who is in his immediate family, he might include his children, whom he continues to see, but not his ex-wife. Thus, after divorce, mother, father, and children each may have a different conception of who is in their immediate family. In fact, one can no longer define "the family" or "the immediate family" except in relation to a particular person.

The situation becomes more complicated in a remarriage that in-

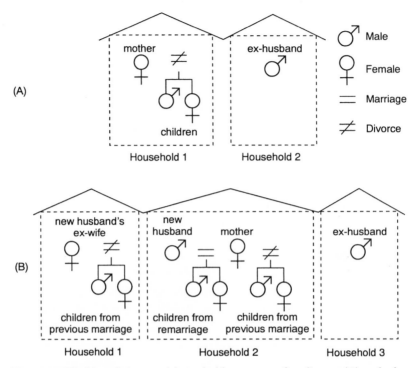

*Figure 3-2.* Kinship relations and household structure after divorce (A) and after the mother's remarriage (B).

volves children from previous marriages. Let us suppose that the mother remarries someone who also has children from a previous marriage and that the mother then has additional children with her new spouse, as diagramed in panel B of Figure 3-2. Now the mother's household contains persons in four different positions—the mother herself, the father/stepfather, the children from her first marriage, and the children from her remarriage. The persons in each of these four positions may have a different conception of who is in their family. The children from the remarriage are likely to include all the members of their household and no one else. The mother's new husband may well include three sets of children: those from his previous marriage, from his new marriage, and from his wife's previous marriage. In reality, few remarriages involve family structures this complex; just 6 percent of remarried couples under age 40 in 1980 had three sets of children.[47] But whenever children are present from previous marriages, multiple definitions arise.

A household formed by divorce or remarriage that involves children from a previous marriage becomes the intersection of an overlapping set of relationships, each of which constitutes an immediate family for one or more members of the household. Although each person in a post-divorce household may have a clear idea of who belongs to his or her immediate family, the definitions of the immediate family are likely to vary widely among persons in the same structural positions in different households.

It also is unclear exactly who a person's more distant relatives are. In many households linked by the ties of broken marriages, there can be considerable interaction among people whose only relationship is through the broken marriage, such as between a husband's second wife and his ex-wife's second husband. Anthropologist Paul Bohannan has labeled these linked households "divorce chains" and the persons related through the ties of broken marriages "quasi-kin."[48] For example, in panel B of Figure 3-2, the children from the mother's previous marriage might play with the children from her new husband's previous marriage when the husband's children come to visit. Over time, these two sets of children might begin to consider themselves relatives, although they have no formal ties to each other.

In practice, it appears that even ex-spouses who share the task of childrearing often have little to do with each other. Furstenberg and Christine Winquist Nord found surprisingly little coordination and consultation between custodial and noncustodial parents, even when the noncustodial parent saw the child frequently. The dominant style, they state, was more like "parallel parenting" than co-parenting: each parent operated as independently as possible. This strategy served to minimize parental conflict.[49] Similarly, a study of divorced families in Northern California by Stanford University researchers found that, by three-and-one-half years after the separation, the most common pattern of interaction between the parents was "disengaged"—low communication and low conflict.[50]

When at least one spouse has children from a previous marriage, the addition of a new adult to the household alters the entire system of relationships among family members. But our society, oriented toward first marriages, provides little guidance to currently divorced adults, to remarried adults, and to their children as to how they should manage their unfamiliar and complex family lives. The lack of institutional-ized—that is, generally accepted—ways of resolving problems is partic-ularly noticeable for the families of remarriages following divorce.[51] To be sure, many aspects of remarried life are similar to life in a first marriage and are subject to established rules of behavior. And remar-riage itself is an institutionalized solution to the ambiguous status of the divorced parent. But for remarried adults and their children, day-to-day life includes many problems for which institutionalized solutions are just beginning to emerge.

Consider the problem of what a stepchild who calls his father "Dad" should call his stepfather. There is still no general rule, but my obser-vations suggest that the most common answer is to call him by his first name. Note, however, that this practice, if accepted, will institutionalize the ambiguous position of the stepparent. An adult whom a child addresses by his first name is neither a parent nor a stranger. Rather, that adult is more like a friend or a companion. The relationship between stepparents and the stepchildren can vary greatly from family to family. Stepparents must create relationships and negotiate with the biological parents and the stepchildren what each person's rights and obligations will be. Consequently, during the first year or two of a remarriage, adults must work carefully and gradually at establishing a coherent system of relationships among kin, step-kin, and quasi-kin.

The first years of life in a stepfamily are also a time of adjustment for children. Many have adapted painfully but successfully to the de-parture of the father from the household. The arrival of a stepfather necessitates further adjustment. One might think that children's psy-chological well-being would improve quickly, because stepfathers can provide the family with additional income, emotional support, warmth, and discipline. But studies show that the overall level of well-being of children in stepfamilies is about the same as that of children living with their mothers.[52]

Among children who have not yet entered adolescence, the addition of a stepfather to the home appears to create more problems for girls than for boys. In contrast, the behavior of young boys seems to improve, or at least doesn't deteriorate, when their mothers remarry.[53] These sex differences are just the opposite of what occurs, according to the psychological studies at least, when marriages break up and young children remain with their mothers alone: boys show more behavior problems and girls are perhaps more depressed and withdrawn. Hetherington and her collaborators speculate that young girls, who tend to form close relationships with their divorced mothers, may view the stepfather as intruders. Young boys, who are more likely to engage in persistent "coercive cycles" of bad behavior with non-remarried mothers, may benefit from the introduction of a stepfather.

In one study of children aged six to nine in stepfamilies, the authors report that boys were doing better when there was more cohesion and emotional bonding between their mothers and their stepfathers, which presumably reflected a greater integration of the stepfather into the life of the family. But girls were doing better when there was *less* cohesion and bonding between the mother and stepfather. The authors argue that the involvement of the stepfather threatens the close relationship that daughters have developed with their mothers.[54] Moreover, several studies have found evidence that children appear to fare better when they are in the custody of the same-sex parent—boys with their fathers, and girls with their mothers.[55] But fathers have custody of their children rarely and often under special circumstances, such as when the mother is unfit or the father has been unusually involved in childrearing. So it is very risky to generalize from the existing studies of same-sex custody.

A recent study of somewhat older children by Hetherington and her collaborators reported that both boys and girls had persistent difficulties in adjusting to the presence of a stepfather. The researchers followed nine-to-thirteen-year-old children in recently formed stepfamilies for two years. They speculated that the developmental tasks of early adolescence—particularly coming to terms with emerging sexuality and developing a sense of autonomy—may make the addition of a stepfather to the home problematic for boys and girls. It may be unavoidably distressing, they argue, for an early adolescent to think of his or her mother and stepfather as sexually active.[56]

It also appears that the role of the stepmother is more problematic than the role of the stepfather. Stepmothers have more competition from absent mothers than stepfathers do from absent fathers because absent mothers are less likely to withdraw from their children's lives. In the NSC, the small number of children in father-custody homes reported substantially more contact with their absent mothers than did children in mother-custody homes with their absent fathers.[57] It may be more difficult, then, for stepmothers to establish a workable role in the family. And because of the selective nature of father custody, children in stepmother-father families may be more troubled. That is, children sometimes may be sent to live with their fathers when their problems are greater than the mother feels she can deal with. In the National Health Interview Survey, parents in stepmother-father families were more likely to feel that their child needed psychological help than were parents in mother-stepfather families.[58] Regardless, there are far fewer resident stepmothers than stepfathers because most mothers retain custody of their children. In 1985 there were 740,000 children under 18 living with a stepmother and a biological father, compared to 6.05 million children who were living with a biological mother and a stepfather.[59]

Finally, the divorce rate for remarried persons is modestly but consistently higher than for persons in first marriages, largely because of the sharply higher risk of divorce during the first few years. Some observers believe that the rate is higher because the remarried population contains a higher proportion of people who, for one reason or another, are likely to resort to divorce if their marriage falters.[60] Furstenberg and Graham Spanier argue, more specifically, that the experience of divorce makes people more averse to remaining in a second unhappy marriage.[61] These arguments were raised initially in reaction to a hypothesis of mine, namely that many of the difficulties of families of remarriage, including the higher divorce rate, stem from the lack of institutionalized support. Without accepted guidelines, solving everyday problems can engender conflict and confusion among family members.[62] The evidence tying second divorces to the incomplete institutionalization of remarriage is mixed, however, and a lesser aversion to divorce among remarried partners is undoubtedly a factor.[63]

## Costs and Benefits

Because of the rise in divorce, more and more people—currently more than one million couples per year—are experiencing the distress of marital separation. Yet the process of divorce does benefit many adults who go through it, because it frees them from the tensions of an unhappy marriage. Most divorced persons say that their lives would have been worse had they not separated from their spouses.[64] At least one partner in every disrupted marriage chooses to divorce and, as best we can judge, the benefits of divorce to that partner outweigh the costs. I suspect, however, that few adults who are about to separate are prepared for the intense emotional difficulties that often are experienced by both partners during the first years after separation or for the economic decline that afflicts many mothers. Most divorced adults will spend most of the rest of their lives not living alone or in a single-parent family but in a family of remarriage. Although parents and children in a family of remarriage can have difficulty adjusting to their complex and poorly institutionalized situation, remarriage improves the financial situation of single parents, creates an additional set of kin to supplement the remaining ties to the kin of noncustodial parents, and can provide another stable source of affection and emotional support.

The situation of children whose parents divorce is more problematic. With few exceptions, children do not want their parents to separate. Yet children's problems often precede the breakup; and some of these problems would have occurred even if the parents had stayed together. Several collaborators and I studied the statistical records of national samples of children in the United States and Great Britain who were followed for four or five years.[65] The records contained information on behavior problems, reading and mathematics achievement, and family difficulties for the children, all of whom were living with two married, biological parents at the beginning of the study. We tracked them as they split into two groups as the years passed: those whose parents divorced and those whose parents stayed together. As might be expected, the children whose parents divorced showed more behavior problems and scored lower on reading and mathematics tests than did the children whose parents stayed together. But when we looked backward through the records to the start of the study—before anyone's parents had separated or divorced—we found that the children whose parents would later divorce *already* were showing more problems and doing worse in reading and mathematics. For boys, we found that about half of what appeared to be the effect of divorce could be predicted on the basis of the boy's problems and his family's difficulties before the break-up. For girls, less of the effect could be predicted beforehand.

These findings suggest that the process of divorce often begins well before the parents split up. Children caught in the conflict preceding a divorce tend to develop problems even while both parents are still in the home. Moreover, the findings suggest that some two-parent families may function poorly, due to serious problems of the parents or the children, regardless of whether the parents ever consider divorce. But these troubled families are invisible to the outside world unless the parents split up—at which point we may mistakenly attribute all of the children's problems to the break-up itself.

Does this mean that parents in troubled marriages needn't stay together for the sake of the children? I think that statement, although true at the extreme, is too simplistic. It is probably true that children are better off, as many researchers have claimed, living with one separated parent than living in a home torn apart by intense conflict or abuse. What if, however, the parents are unhappy with their marriage, have lost much of their affection for or interest in one another, but are able to limp along without much hostility or open conflict? No one knows how many divorcing couples are in this situation, and I don't think a divorce under these conditions helps children. Moreover, Wallerstein and Kelly found that some partners in conflict-ridden marriages still were able to share in maintaining a loving and supportive relationship with their children. Even though many of the children in their study doubted that their parents were happily married, even though many were well aware of a long history of difficulties between their parents, very few greeted divorce with relief; most were shocked and distressed at the news that their parents were separating.[66]

I think it is clear that most children do not benefit from divorce. Our

U. S. and British study suggests that overall the effect on children of the break-up and its aftermath is negative but modest in size. For example, children whose parents divorced during the study showed about 5 to 20 percent more behavior problems, once their pre-divorce characteristics were taken into account.[67] A review of ninety-two studies, by Paul R. Amato and Bruce Kieth, concluded: "Parental divorce (or the factors associated with it) lowers the well-being of children. However, the estimated effects are generally weak."[68] These averages, however, conceal wide variations in children's responses. I think the data suggest that most children suffer only moderately increased difficulties; some do better than before the break-up; and some experience serious, long-lasting problems. There also may be long-term effects that show up only in adulthood. And the evidence reviewed in this chapter suggests that, despite the material advantages that a parental remarriage usually provides, remarriage can cause further difficulties in children's adjustment, at least in the short term.

In the first edition of this book, I closed this chapter by speculating that the degree of difficulty experienced by adults and children in single-parent and stepparent families might be reduced in the 1980s. I argued that many of the problems of single and remarried parents can be traced to the lack of generally accepted guidelines for behavior in these kinds of families. I suggested that the slowing of the rate of increase in divorce in the late 1970s might provide a respite from rapid change, a period in which adjustments could be made:

> The sharp increases in divorce and remarriage since 1960 mean that many more Americans than ever before are grappling with the special problems of family life after divorce and after remarriage. With greater numbers, the amount of communication among these families has increased. In the past few years, several associations of divorced and remarried parents have been formed, and numerous newsletters, pamphlets, and books have appeared. I think it likely that these families will generate ways of resolving common problems which will come to be widely accepted as standards of conduct . . . If so, family life after divorce and remarriage may be somewhat easier to manage than it is today.

I still find that argument plausible, but its predictions were wrong. In the decade between editions of this book, despite all the activity and research and attention to these matters and despite a leveling off of the divorce rate, divorce and remarriage did not become any easier for parents and children—at least as far as I can tell. The widespread sharing of the experience of divorce did not assuage the personal pain adults and children feel when a family breaks up. It did not lead to much improvement in the precarious economic situation many divorced mothers find themselves in. And it could not substitute for the lengthy period of adjustment to the break-up of a family or to the presence of a new stepparent. This lack of progress tempers my optimism about whether it will be easier to manage these transitions a decade from now.

# 4

# Race and Poverty

So far, I have discussed trends in family patterns for the American population as a whole, rather than examining the changing behavior of the many ethnic, regional, religious, and social class groups. There is reason to believe that the postwar trends have been parallel for most of these groups.[1] Yet one set of group differences deserves separate consideration: those between the typical family patterns of blacks and of whites.[2] Some of these differences—in out-of-wedlock childbearing and in household structure, for instance—appear to have existed for at least a century. Most of the postwar trends examined in previous chapters appear to have moved in the same direction for both blacks and whites. Black fertility, for example, peaked in the late 1950s just as white fertility did, and both black and white fertility subsequently declined. There was a short surge in divorce among blacks immediately after World War II, just as for whites. And rates of separation and divorce increased at about the same speed for both groups between 1960 and 1980.[3] But in other important ways—such as the proportion of men and women ever marrying and the ages at which women bear children—the family lives of blacks and whites have diverged since World War II.

Poverty among both blacks and whites has become increasingly concentrated in the growing number of households maintained by unmarried women, their children, and other relatives. These households are usually called "female-headed families," and I will sometimes employ this common usage. But this census-based definition assumes that families never extend over more than one household—a problematic assumption for black families. In the late 1940s, 15 percent of the poorest fifth of all families in the United States were headed by a woman under 65; in the mid-1980s, 35 percent were headed by a woman under 65.[4] These female-headed families remain poor for a longer time than do low-income two-parent families. Consider the evidence from the Panel Study of Income Dynamics (PSID). Greg J. Duncan looked at information collected between 1969 and 1978 and isolated two groups of low-income families: the "temporarily poor," whose income fell below the poverty line only one or two years during the ten-year period, and the much smaller group of "persistently poor," whose incomes fell below the line at least eight of the ten years. He found that most temporarily poor families had an adult male in the household, but 61 percent of the persistently poor families were female-headed. Duncan also found that, regardless of household structure, most of the temporarily poor were white, but 62 percent of the persistently poor were black. Households that were both black and female-headed constituted 31 percent of the persistently poor.[5]

In this chapter I will examine the connections among race and poverty and the family. To do so I must focus on the differences, rather than the similarities, between black and white families and must make both positive and negative judgments. Over the past few decades, the research literature on black families has gone from a critical perspective to one that emphasizes strengths.[6] Both perspectives, once they are stripped of their rhetorical excesses, are instructive. I will argue that in order to fully understand what has happened over the past few decades, it is necessary to accept aspects of both views. The strengths of black extended families have enabled parents and children to survive tough times. But some of the very adaptations that provide a measure of protection to family members have made it more difficult for them to escape from poverty.

## Divergent Trends

No trend illustrates more clearly the divergence in black and white family patterns than the changing timing of marriage. In the late nineteenth century—the earliest period for which we have reliable information—and throughout the first half of the twentieth century, blacks tended to marry at a younger age than did whites. Between 1940 and 1950, however, the average age at which whites married began to decrease, and by mid-century there was little difference between the two groups. Figure 4-1 displays the percentage of white and nonwhite women aged twenty to twenty-four who were single (that is, never-married) in a given year.[7] Around the turn of the century this percentage was much greater for white women, but by 1950 the difference had disappeared.

After 1950 the trends turned around. The percentage single dropped further for white women in the 1950s, as more of them married earlier. But for nonwhites the percentage single rose during the 1950s and has continued to rise ever since, with the sharpest increase coming in the 1970s. In 1990, despite the movement toward later marriage among

*Figure 4-1.* Percentage never married for women aged 20–24, by color, 1890–1989. Sources: for 1890–1940, Paul Jacobson, *American Marriage and Divorce* (New York: Rinehart, 1959), p. 62. For 1950–1970, U.S. Bureau of the Census, *U.S. Census of Population: 1950*, vol. 4, Special Reports, pt. 2, chap. D, tables 1 and 2; *U.S. Census of Population: 1960*, vol. 1, Characteristics of the Population, pt. 1: U.S. Summary, table 1976; and *U.S. Census of Population: 1970*, vol. 1, Characteristics of the Population, pt. 1: U.S. Summary, sec. 2, table 203. For 1980 and 1989, U.S. Bureau of the Census, *Current Population Reports,* Series P-20, no. 445, "Marital Status and Living Arrangements: March 1989."

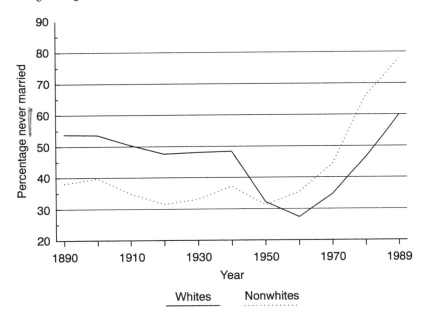

whites since 1960, the percentage single among nonwhite women exceeded the percentage single among white women—76 percent versus 60 percent for those aged twenty to twenty-four. Since World War II, then, a historical difference between blacks and whites in marriage timing has been turned on its head: blacks used to marry earlier than whites, but now they marry later.

They are increasingly less likely to ever marry. In the next decades the percentage of women ever marrying in the population as a whole may drop a point or two below the historical minimum of 90 percent. The figure for black women has been below this number for several decades, and the gap between blacks and whites has widened. Figure 4-2 displays estimates by Neil G. Bennett, David E. Bloom, and Patricia H. Craig of the proportion of white and black women in four birth cohorts who will ever marry. Among the most recent cohort, women born in the 1950s, these estimates suggest that 91 percent of the whites,

*Figure 4-2.* Estimated percentage who will ever marry for four birth cohorts of women, by race. Source: Neil G. Bennett, David E. Bloom, and Patricia H. Craig, "The Divergence of Black and White Marriage Patterns," *American Journal of Sociology* 95 (November 1989): 692–722, table 1.

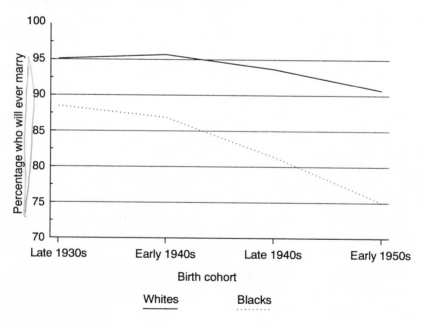

but only 75 percent of the blacks, will ever marry.[8] Another recent study estimates that only 70 percent of black women will ever marry.[9]

In addition, black marriages break up more often than white marriages; blacks who are separated are less likely to obtain a legal divorce than are whites; and blacks who are divorced are increasingly less likely to remarry than are whites. For instance, the rates of marriage and divorce in the period 1965 to 1979 indicated that 47 percent of all black married women would be separated or divorced within ten years of marriage, compared to 28 percent of non-Hispanic whites and 26 percent of Mexican Americans. Among the separated, only 55 percent of black women would obtain a divorce within four years of their separation, compared to 94 percent of non-Hispanic whites and 78 percent of Mexican Americans. And among all separated and divorced women, only 32 percent of black women would remarry within ten years of their separation, compared to 72 percent of non-Hispanic whites and 53 percent of Mexican Americans.[10]

Black women, in sum, are less likely to marry, stay married, and remarry. Those who marry do so at an older age than do whites. The differences between blacks and whites in the timing of marriage, the lifetime chance of ever marrying, and the chance of a divorced woman ever remarrying are greater than they were a generation ago. As a result, black women spend far less of their life in a marriage than do white women. A recent estimate of the proportion of their lifetime that white women can expect to spend in an intact marriage or a remarriage indicated that the percentage declined from 54 percent at the rates prevalent in 1945–1950 to 43 percent at the rates of 1975–1980.[11] This is a certainly a large change; it means that white women now can expect to spend less than half of their lives married.[12] But among black women the corresponding figure has plunged from 40 percent to 22 percent— about the same proportion of life that the average college-educated person spends attending school. Marriage has become just a temporary stage of life for blacks, preceded by a lengthening period of singlehood and followed by a long period of living without a spouse. Some of that time is commonly spent in cohabiting relationships, but these relationships tend to be relatively short. For blacks, even more so than for whites, a long, stable marriage is the exception rather than the rule.

The racial trends in childbearing are more complex. Black and white women have become more alike in the number of children they bear over their lifetimes but less alike in when they have them. To understand this story, let us begin in the 1950s, when black and white women had children at similar ages but otherwise contributed to the baby boom in different ways.[13] An exceptionally high percentage of white women—more than nine in ten—had at least one child, and completed family sizes increased moderately. Among black women, a lower percentage had at least one child, but those who had children at all had substantially larger families—more than one additional child, on average.

Then, starting in the 1960s, white women began to postpone having children until older ages much more so than did black women. Moreover, the proportion of women having children at all declined more rapidly among whites than among blacks.[14] By the 1980s, the average age at childbirth was about three years older among white mothers than among black mothers; and estimates suggested that a lower percentage of white women would ever have at least one child.[15] Because black women, on average, had their first births at younger ages than whites, one might expect black families to exceed white families in size. But that wasn't the case. Between the 1950s and the 1980s another change had occurred: the completed family sizes of black women who had at least one child dropped more sharply than among whites. So by the 1980s, the overall levels of fertility were similar for blacks and whites (see Figure 1-4). These similar levels of fertility, however, were achieved in different ways. Black women, on average, began having children at earlier ages than whites and stopped at earlier ages.

Whites, then, have postponed both marriage and childbearing over the past few decades, whereas blacks have postponed marriage even more but childbearing much less. These developments have led to what is perhaps the most striking difference between the current family patterns of blacks and whites: a far higher proportion of black children are born to young, unmarried mothers than is the case for white children. Figure 4-3 compares the age and marital status of the white and black mothers of children born in 1988. It shows that 1 out of 5 black children was born to an unmarried teenager. Another 1 out of 5 was born to an unmarried woman age 20 to 24. The comparable proportions for whites were about 1 out of 18 and 1 out of 16,

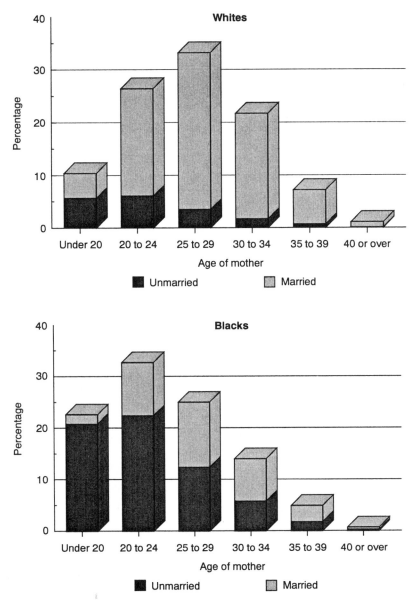

*Figure 4-3.* Distribution of births in 1988, by age of mother and marital status, for whites and blacks. Source: U.S. National Center for Health Statistics, *Monthly Vital Statistics Report*, vol. 39, no. 4, Supplement, "Advance Report of Final Natality Statistics, 1988" (Washington: U.S. Government Printing Office, 1990), tables 2 and 18.

respectively. Overall in 1988, 64 percent of all black births occurred out of wedlock, compared to 18 percent of all white births.[16]

It is commonly thought that this dramatic rise in the proportion of black children born out of wedlock is the result of a sharp increase in childbearing among unmarried black women. Surprisingly, this is not so. Unmarried black teenagers and unmarried black women age 20 to 24 were no more likely to give birth in the late 1980s than they were in the late 1960s.[17] Then what caused the increased proportion of out-of-wedlock births? The answer is twofold: First, births among black *married* women fell sharply during the 1960s and early 1970s and then leveled off. Second, during the entire period, fewer and fewer young black women married.[18] As the ranks of the unmarried grew, the proportion of children they produced also grew, even though the likelihood that an individual would bear a child in a given year did not change much. Marriage has virtually disappeared among black teenagers: in 1989, only 4 percent of black 18-and-19-year-old women had ever married.[19] And it was rare in 1988 for a black teenage mother to marry the father of her child before giving birth; less than one in ten did so.[20]

To be sure, the trends among young white women have been in the same direction. The birth rate for unmarried white women has in fact risen since the 1960s[21] (although the birth rate among black unmarried teenagers is still nearly four times higher than among white teenagers). But the movement away from marriage has not been as pronounced among young whites. In 1989, 11 percent of white 18-and-19-year-old women were married, and in 1988 nearly half of white teenage mothers married the father of their child before giving birth.[22] Moreover, the decline in marriage among young black women had a much greater impact on overall black fertility trends because so many more black children are born to young mothers.

In sum, the divergence between blacks and whites in marriage and in the timing of births has been substantial, and it has caused profound differences in the family lives of black and white children. Census Bureau data collected in 1989 for children living with at least one parent show the following: black children are about half as likely as white children to be living with both parents or with one parent and a stepparent (41 percent versus 81 percent); they are about eight times

more likely to be living with a never-married parent (31 percent versus
4 percent); and they are more than half again as likely to be living with
a separated or divorced parent (25 percent versus 14 percent). The most
common arrangement for black children under age six—applying to 42
percent of them—was to live with a never-married mother.[23]

## The Marriage Market

There is much debate, and considerable uncertainty, about the causes
of this divergence in the family lives of blacks and whites. Some of it
centers on the marriage market—the process by which men and women
search for spouses. The best-known model of the marriage market was
developed by the economist Gary Becker. Borrowing from the theory
of international trade, Becker treated persons searching for marriage
partners as if they were nations searching for trading partners. Two key
goods were being traded: income and "household production," the
latter including the bearing and rearing of children and housework.
Women, Becker argued, have a comparative advantage in household
production: it is more efficient, relative to their ability to earn wages,
for them to do it than for men. In turn, men have a comparative
advantage in earning wages. Therefore, both men and women benefit
economically if they marry and each specializes—the husband working
for wages, the wife doing the childrearing and the housework. [24]

Becker's model works best as an explanation for the sharp division
of labor between husbands and wives in the 1950s, when few married
women were employed outside the home. Indeed, the model is partly
a formalization of the argument that Talcott Parsons developed in the
1940s and 1950s to explain the prevalence of the breadwinner-homemaker family.[25] It may seem dated in the 1990s, when a majority of
wives work outside the home. Yet it offers an explanation of why
marriage as an institution seems to be in decline: as women's earning
power has increased, the gains achieved by marrying and then special-
izing in household production have decreased.

Does it apply to the black marriage market? In 1940, six out of ten
employed black women were working as domestics, cleaning the homes
and doing the laundry of whites. It was low-paying, often demeaning

work, but it was available and it was all that many black women could get. Over the past few decades, however, as discrimination has lessened, the barriers to better jobs for black women have crumbled. The proportion of employed black women who work in white-collar jobs increased from 7 percent in 1940 to 51 percent in 1980. By 1980, black women earned as much as white women with the same amount of schooling—a monumental change from mid-century.[26] It is also true that, on average, black women still earn less than black men, just as white women earn less than white men. But the gender gap has closed dramatically for blacks. In 1954, the average earnings of black women employed full-time were only 58 percent of the earnings of black men employed full-time; thirty years later the figure was 86 percent.[27] The narrowing is due in part to the labor market gains of black women and in part to the labor market losses of black men. Under current circumstances, then, black women have less to gain by trading household services for the income of a husband. The gains-to-trade model predicts a decrease in the proportion ever marrying as well as an increase in divorce and separation.[28]

Becker and other observers have argued that government social welfare programs have increased women's economic independence and correspondingly decreased the motivation to marry for poor blacks and whites alike. It is likely, they suggest, that the greater availability and increased benefits of public assistance encouraged or enabled more single-parent families to exist. Charles Murray pointed out that from the mid-1960s to the early 1970s both the percentage of children living in female-headed households and the percentage of children whose families were receiving welfare benefits (Aid to Families with Dependent Children) rose sharply.[29]

David T. Ellwood and Lawrence H. Summers noted, however, that the percentage of children living in female-headed households has continued to increase since the mid-1970s, even though the percentage receiving welfare has not. In fact, the real value of AFDC benefits declined in the 1970s, because federal and state governments did not provided cost-of-living increases; yet the upward trend in single-parent households continued.[30] Other empirical studies suggest that increased welfare benefits have a modest effect at most on the proportion of single-parent households, although the effect may have increased some-what in the 1980s.[31] Nevertheless, it is possible that welfare benefits reached a minimally adequate threshold in the late 1960s and helped trigger a change in family structure.

But whether the focus is on earnings or welfare payments, the gains-to-trade model has limitations. It assumes that the black and white marriage markets operate the same way, but in some key respects they do not. For instance, the model predicts that women who are employed will be less eager to marry because they have less to gain economically. One might expect, then, that fewer employed women will be married. That is true for whites but false for blacks, as information about women aged 25 to 34 in the March 1988 Current Population Survey shows. Among whites, as the model predicts, only 62 percent of those who _White_ were employed had ever married, compared to 79 percent of those who were not in the labor force. Among blacks, however, 32 percent of _Black_ employed women had ever married, compared to 27 percent of those not in the labor force.[32] Moreover, separated and divorced black women with more education (an indicator of earning potential) are more likely to remarry, whereas education is unrelated to whether white women remarry.[33] It may be that black men, as a result of their lower earnings, have a stronger preference for working wives than do white men. And I think it likely that African American culture has been more accepting of working wives.

The black and white marriage markets also differ in other respects. In most marriages, black or white, the spouses have similar levels of education. But when differences exist, white women, as the model predicts, tend to marry men who have more education—and so more earning potential—than they do, whereas black women tend to marry men with less education. The differences are modest and appear to be decreasing over time, but they have been noted consistently.[34] Another related contrast: white women who have attended college are less likely to marry than are those who have not; yet black women who have attended college are more likely to marry than are those who have not—despite the short supply of college-educated black men.[35]

No one knows exactly why the black and white marriage markets are different, but I think much of the explanation lies in the greater need among blacks to pool incomes—either between a husband and wife or among a network of kin—and the long tradition among blacks of female employment. Because the incomes of black workers have been far below those of whites and unemployment has been far higher, black families have long needed more than one income to survive. Black women historically have worked in larger numbers than white women. The labor market niche black women occupied as domestics provided more reliable, if low-paying, employment than black men could find. It is only recently that the proportion of employed women among whites has caught up with the proportion among blacks.[36] Whereas white men and women may have sought traditionally to trade income for household services, blacks sought to combine incomes. The expectation that women will work has long been a part of African American culture. Consequently, women with higher earning potential make more attractive marriage partners. Perhaps the same pattern will emerge in the white marriage market as employment becomes the norm for married women.

A related set of explanations for the sharp decrease in marriage among blacks centers on the relative numbers of women and men in the marriage market. According to a 1989 survey of Los Angeles area residents, black women perceive the marriage market to be tighter than do whites or Latinos. Sixty-nine percent of black women responded that there were not enough men like themselves, compared to 59 percent of white women and 54 percent of Latino women. In contrast, 58 percent of black men thought there were more than enough women like themselves, compared to 42 percent of white men and 39 percent of Latino men.[37]

Historically in the United States, the number of men per 100 women—which demographers refer to as the sex ratio—has been lower for blacks than for whites.[38] In 1980 there were 97 black men per 100 black women at ages 20 to 24, compared to 102 men per 100 women among whites.[39] The greater shortage among blacks derives from their slightly lower sex ratio at birth and from higher male mortality at younger ages. The shortage at birth is presumably of biological origin. But the higher mortality is of social origin—a function of poorer health and, more recently, an extremely high level of violent death. At the rates prevalent in 1988, for example, about 1 out of 100 black 15-year-old boys will die at his own or another's hand before he reaches age 25; of the survivors, another 1 out of 100 will die violently before age 35.[40] The overall racial difference, however, is hardly enough to account for the large differentials in marriage behavior between black and white young adults. The sex ratio changed very little for either blacks or whites between 1970 and 1980; yet marriage rates declined for both groups and the racial divergence in marriage behavior widened.[41] Consequently, the recent decline in marriage among blacks and the growing marriage gap between blacks and whites cannot be explained by the sex ratio in a strict demographic sense.

Nevertheless, there are other social and economic factors which may have reduced the number of black men who are attractive marriage partners for black women. First, black men are more likely to marry white women than black women are to marry white men;[42] and intermarriage, though still uncommon, has increased rapidly. Whereas just 1 percent of black men who married for the first time in 1959 wed a white woman, 5 percent of black men who married for the first time in 1979, the last year for which information is available, did so. In contrast, only 1 percent of never-married black women wed white men in 1979.[43] So intermarriage removes about 5 out of every 100 black men—but only 1 out of every 100 black women—from the black first marriage market. The net loss of 4 out of 100 males makes the current market tighter for black women. And there are other, grimmer reasons why the pool of eligible black males may have diminished: high and often growing rates of incarceration and institutionalization.[44] In the 1970s and 1980s, when the prison population expanded greatly, nearly half of all inmates were black. On any given day, about 3 out of every 100 black men in their twenties are behind bars.[45] In addition, perhaps 1 out of 100 black men between the ages of 18 and 44 are admitted to state and county mental hospitals each year.[46] Finally, an unknown number of unmarried men are incapacitated by drug addiction or alcoholism.

A number of experts have argued that fewer black women are marrying because fewer black men earn enough to support a family. For example, between 1969 and 1984, there was a sharp decline in the number of young adult black men who worked at all. The proportion of 25-to-34-year-old black men who earned any money during the year dropped from 93 percent to 85 percent; in contrast, the comparable figures for whites declined only from 97 percent to 96 percent. The decline was sharpest for high school drop-outs (from 93 percent to 77 percent) but it was substantial among high school graduates (from 95 to 87 percent) as well.[47] To take this decline into account, several researchers have developed more refined sex ratios. For example, William Julius Wilson and Kathryn M. Neckerman reported that the ratios of employed young adult men per 100 women were similar for whites and blacks until the mid-1960s; then this index fell more sharply for blacks than for whites. The authors maintain that after the mid-1960s it was increasingly more difficult for black women than for white women to find a suitable—meaning employed—man to marry.[48] Another recent study analyzed Census Bureau data on metropolitan labor markets. The simple ratio of men to women in the labor markets had little effect on marriage rates, but women were more likely to marry in markets where young men had more economic opportunities. Nevertheless, black women still had substantially lower marriage rates even after controls for labor market conditions.[49]

Wilson and others have argued further that the declining employment prospects for less-educated black men are a result of broad changes in the economy.[50] As the economy has shifted from producing manufactured goods to producing services, the demand for factory workers has declined. The number of decent-paying blue-collar jobs that less-educated men could obtain has dwindled, as the jobs have gone to Japan, Korea, or Brazil. The expanding service sector is said to offer either low-paying jobs such as restaurant work or jobs that require higher education, such as computer programming, but not much in between. Factories and offices have moved to the suburbs, far from black neighborhoods in the inner city.[51]

These arguments are quite plausible, and many observers agree that the decline in demand for semi-skilled workers has been an important factor in explaining the decline in marriage. Certainly, the earnings of young black men with little education have fallen sharply. In fact, the slide has been so steep for men aged 25 to 34 that high school graduates in 1984 were earning less than high school drop-outs fifteen years earlier.[52] During the 1970s and 1980s the earnings gap between well-educated and poorly educated black men widened. Although black college graduates were doing better, relative to whites, than ever before, black high school drop-outs were doing worse. Between 1969 and 1984, the proportion of black men aged 25 to 44 reporting incomes over $25,000 and the proportion reporting incomes less than $5,000 *both* increased.[53] Whether this divergence is caused by the movement of jobs overseas or the rise of the service sector or some other, poorly understood forces is difficult to determine. In any case, for both blacks and whites, wealthier families have been growing even wealthier in recent years whereas poorer families have been growing poorer.

But direct evidence linking declining job opportunities to falling marriage rates among blacks is surprisingly thin. Several statistical studies have found that, although changes in employment made a difference, the changes did not account for much of the decline in marriage over time. Robert Mare and Christopher Winship compared persons who married versus those who remained single in the 1940, 1950, 1960, 1970, and 1980 Censuses and in Current Population Surveys (conducted by the Bureau of the Census) in the mid-1980s. They found that an unmarried man who was employed was more likely to marry. But they also concluded that "recent declines in employment rates among young blacks are simply not large enough to account for a substantial part of the trend in their marriage rates."[54] Ellwood and David T. Rodda reached similar conclusions using information from a national study that followed young men for several years.[55] Another study examined declines in marriage in the PSID between two periods, 1974 to 1980 and 1981 to 1987. The decline in young black men's labor market prospects appeared to account for only about one-fourth of the decrease in marriage among black women.[56]

Other evidence shows that the deteriorating labor market position of poorly educated young black men cannot be the only reason why fewer blacks are marrying. During the 1960s and 1970s, marriage declined nearly as much among better-off blacks as among poor blacks. For example, Robert Lerman calculated that between 1970 and 1980, the proportion of black high school drop-outs who hadn't married by age 29 rose from 24 to 38 percent—consistent with the deteriorating labor market explanations. But the proportion unmarried at 29 rose from 19 to 30 percent among high school graduates and from 19 to 29 percent among those who had attended college.[57] So the fall in marriage was nearly as large among better-educated blacks as among the high school drop-outs. Something else must have influenced the behavior of better-educated blacks. Similarly, steadily employed black men—who are attractive marriage partners and are in relatively short supply—should have high marriage rates.[58] But marriage has declined sharply among this group as well. Christopher Jencks reported that between 1960 and 1980 the decline in the number of 35-to-44-year-old black men who were married and living with their wives was nearly as large among men who were year-round full-time workers as among all blacks in that age range.[59]

Further evidence that economics is far from the whole story comes from a 1986 survey of residents of poor, inner-city Chicago neighborhoods. Among men in the survey who had fathered a child out of wedlock prior to ever marrying, those who were employed at the time of the survey were nearly twice as likely to have married the mother of their child after the birth. Without doubt, then, employment had a lot to do with the men's propensity to marry. But strong differences remained among men of different racial and ethnic groups—all of whom lived in poor neighborhoods. Even after controlling for employment and education, non-Hispanic whites were four times as likely to have married the mother of their child after the birth than were blacks; and Mexican men were more than twice as likely to have married than were blacks.[60]

In addition, the racial differences between white and black women in out-of-wedlock childbearing and subsequent marriage exist at all educational levels. The 1980 Census data on never-married women aged 18 to 34 show the expected racial difference among women who hadn't graduated from high school: blacks were four to six times more likely to have had a child. But among similar women with college degrees, the contrast also was sharp: 11 percent of blacks had borne a child, compared to less than 1 percent of whites.[61] In fact, the June 1980 Current Population Survey shows that one out of five black female college graduates had given birth before they were married; the figure for non-Hispanic white college graduates was one out of 50.[62] Similarly, tabulations of 1980 Census data by Reynolds Farley and Walter R. Allen demonstrate that the racial differences in family structure hold at all income levels. For example, 2 percent of white families with incomes of $50,000 and over were female-headed, compared to 11 percent of black families. Comparisons based on education and occupation, the authors of this study write, also show pervasive differences across all social class categories.[63]

What conclusions can be drawn about the importance of the marriage market from all of this somewhat contradictory evidence? I would draw two: First, the forces of the market—some combination of the increasing earnings of black women; the continuing employment problems of black men; the higher rate of out-marriage among black men; the toll of violence, imprisonment, and drugs; and perhaps the expansion of welfare in the late 1960s and early 1970s—contributed to the dramatic decline of marriage among blacks. Second, trends in employment and income cannot explain most of the decline. To be sure, at any point in time, black men (and women) who are employed are more likely to marry. But over the past few decades, the flight from marriage has occurred among employed and better-educated blacks as well. (It also has occurred among whites, but not to the same degree.) And it does not appear that changes in employment and income among blacks were large enough to account for the massive decline in marriage.

## History and Culture

The persistence of racial differences in family patterns—even after employment and earnings are considered—suggests that for a complete explanation one must look beyond economics to history and culture. In 1982, Frank Furstenberg and I visited a senior citizens' center in a black neighborhood of an eastern city as part of a study of American grandparents. There we talked with a group of black grandmothers, many of whom had lived with their grandchildren and had helped with the childrearing. These grandmothers exercised authority, mixed with love, in ways that few white grandmothers could match. One woman told us: "I was always named 'sergeant'—'Here comes the sergeant.' I loved them [her grandchildren]. I *did* for them, and gave to them, so that they had an education, so that they had a trade. I went to school regularly to check on them; they didn't know I was coming."[64] Furstenberg and I went on to conduct a national survey of grandparents, and our findings confirmed that black grandparents, on average, were more deeply involved in their grandchildren's lives than were white grandparents. You would have to look far and wide before locating a white grandmother who would check on her grandchildren at school without their knowing she was coming. Moreover, the greater involvement of black grandmothers seemed to hold at all income levels, a finding consistent with reports of the importance of extended kin in black middle-class families.[65] We concluded that black grandmothers were a source of strength and support for their children and grandchildren in ways largely unmatched by whites regardless of income.

When Furstenberg and I wrote about the strengths of black families this way, no one seemed to mind that we were bringing in the idea of cultural differences between blacks and whites. Yet in many cases to invoke culture in a discussion of black families is to provoke fierce criticism. The harsh reaction stems from the negative way in which African American culture is sometimes portrayed; in the most unfavorable treatments blacks are said to be trapped in the "culture of poverty," doomed at a young age to life in the lower class. Nevertheless, the issue of cultural differences must be addressed. Economics and social structure cannot explain all of the divergence in marriage patterns between black and white families.

By culture I mean the set of shared understandings that a group has about the nature of a social institution—in this case the family. These understandings shape people's beliefs about what a family does and who is in one. They influence the kinds of households that people form and the amount of assistance they expect from relatives living elsewhere. Culture guides behavior but doesn't determine it, and it often provides more than one model of how to act. Writing about cultural influences on fertility, Susan Greenhalgh observed, "Culture is like a spice rack of ideas and practices from which people choose depending on the menu of opportunities and constraints posed by their environments."[66]

There are longstanding cultural differences in the ways blacks and whites conceive of and carry out their family lives. In particular, African American culture places greater emphasis on ties to a network of kin that can extend over more than one household. Extended kin such as the grandparents, parents, and children Furstenberg and I studied expect to provide and to receive more help from each other than do extended kin in white families. They also live together more often—about half of all middle-aged black women, according to another national study, live in a three-generation household at some point, compared to about one-fifth of white women.[67] But the flip side of this greater emphasis on extended kin is less emphasis on the husband-wife bond.

Several studies going back to at least the late nineteenth century suggest that a network of kin extending across households has been a more important component of family life, and the husband-wife unit a less important component, for blacks than for whites. Jacqueline Jones found that among rural blacks in the late nineteenth and early twentieth centuries, extended kin networks often provided support and assistance to two-parent sharecropper households attempting to eke out a living. She quotes one government researcher's disapproving view of the exchanges among sugar workers in 1902: "They have an unfortunate notion of generosity, which enables the more worthless to borrow fuel, food, and what not on all hands from the more thrifty."[68] In a small black town on Maryland's rural Eastern Shore at the beginning of the twentieth century, extensive kinship ties existed among sixteen of twenty-four housing-lot owners. An aged resident recalled to historian Shepard Krech how, after his father died when he was four and his mother went to Baltimore to find work, he lived with one grandmother, then the other, then his great-grandmother, sometimes eating meals with one and staying at night with another.[69]

Statistical evidence can be found in a study of a large national sample of original manuscript records from the 1910 Census. The analyses of the 1910 sample support two conclusions: that most black households included two parents, but that there were substantial differences between the households of blacks and whites. S. Philip Morgan and his colleagues found that black mothers with children were more than three times as likely to be living without a male partner in the household as were white mothers with children.[70] Higher mortality among blacks undoubtedly accounted for some of the difference; but the researchers found that the racial difference was greatest among younger mothers, who would have been least affected by widowhood. The researchers also found evidence that black children more often were raised by kin other than their parents, even when the parents were still alive: about 7 percent of black children, compared to 2 percent of white children, had mothers who were alive but were not living with them. Even among two-parent households, blacks were four times more likely to have children living elsewhere. Morgan and his colleagues concluded that the family patterns of blacks and whites were substantially different in 1910 in ways that cannot be accounted for simply by differences in fertility and mortality. The differences were pervasive, existing in both rural and urban areas. Black children were more likely to live in mother-headed households, and the greater percentage of children raised by other kin suggests that ties to extended kin networks were more common.

This is not to say that the racial differences in family life in the nineteenth and early twentieth century were as large as they are now—they were not. Herbert G. Gutman examined plantation records, census materials, and other documents, and reported that most slave children grew up in two-parent households. He also found evidence that a high proportion of black households in the late nineteenth and early twentieth centuries contained two parents. Still, the two-parent households, as Gutman himself noted, were embedded in extended families. And he reported higher rates of male-absent households among blacks in turn-of-the-century New York City than among Jews or Italians.[71]

Some of the cultural distinctiveness of black families may extend back to slavery and across the Atlantic to Africa. The extent to which elements of African culture survive among African Americans has been hotly debated, but the similarities are striking.[72] African society traditionally has been organized into lineages, large kinship groups that trace their descent through either male or female lines. Members of the lineage cooperated and shared resources with others. Adults carefully controlled and monitored courtship and marriage among the young; what mattered most was not the happiness of the married couple but rather the birth of children who could be retained by the lineage.

In the West we are used to thinking of marriage as an event that occurs at a particular time: two people participate in a ceremony and register their intentions with the state. But in Africa, marriage was much more of a process, a series of steps that occurred over a long period of time.[73] Childbearing could occur before the ceremony or exchange of gifts, but the clear expectation was that marriage would follow within a few years. The system worked because the families of the young couple monitored and supervised the entire process. If, for example, a woman bore a child but the process later went astray and marriage did not occur, the kin of the woman could protest to the kin of the man, and a dispute over gifts of livestock or rights to the child might arise. Although marital status might at first be ambiguous and subject to different interpretations, the process unfolded under public scrutiny. If disagreements about, say, bridewealth payments become too serious, the families usually had the authority to bring the process to a halt.

When these cultural patterns were brought to the United States by African slaves, the lineages, as anthropologist Niara Sudarkasa has written, were reduced to extended families.[74] The distinction is that in Africa lineage elders had substantial authority over individuals because lineages controlled the allocation of crucial resources, most notably land. A person who was disowned by a lineage faced a terrible future. The extended kin groups in the United States retained the important supportive role of lineages—kin helped each other and shared whatever resources they had. But the authority of the wider kinship group withered because it no longer controlled the allocation of land or livestock or jobs. Thus, the extended kinship groups among many African Americans were limited to being social support networks; extended families were important to the lives of individuals but had less control over their actions. I would speculate that black extended families in cities today may be less effective at supervising the behavior of adolescents than were extended families among land-owning blacks in the nineteenth century or in African lineages.

Gutman, as mentioned earlier, noted the strong ties among extended kin in slave families. Jones wrote that it was socially acceptable among the slave community for a young woman to have her first child out of wedlock. But a long-lasting marriage, she stated, usually followed within a couple of years, although not necessarily to the child's father—a pattern quite similar to customs in some African societies. Moreover, Jones argued that "the outline of African work patterns endured among the slaves."[75] In particular, many West African women had primary responsibility for cultivating food. Under slavery, of course, women were forced to labor in the fields. But even after Emancipation, Jones notes, rural black families depended on the field work of women much more so than white families did.

In summary, black families have long been distinct from white families in ties to extended kin, childbearing prior to marriage, sending children to be raised by other relatives, and women's work outside the home. I have suggested that the distinctiveness is in part a consequence of long-standing cultural patterns that were visible at least a century ago. This still leaves open the question of why, as noted earlier in this chapter, the patterns of marriage and the timing of childbearing of whites and blacks became even less similar in the last half of the twentieth century. There is no doubt that the proximate causes of the recent divergence lie in contemporary American society—something happened over the last few decades that set black and white families on separate courses. The evidence is inconclusive and has been read differently by people with different points of view. Let me add my reading.

What happened in the last half of the twentieth century, I think, was that black families responded to two developments: a society-wide shift in values and a change in the labor market that was particularly damaging to blacks. The society-wide shift was the weakening of the institution of marriage. I have described the rise of cohabitation, the postponement of marriage, the increase in divorce, and the separation of marriage from childbearing that has spread throughout American society since the 1960s. These developments were rooted in the increasing economic independence of men and women, but they also reflected a cultural drift toward a more individualistic ethos, one which emphasizes self-fulfillment in personal relations. It de-emphasizes the obligations people have to others—including their spouses and partners. It allows, even encourages, people to make or break bonds of intimacy as their sense of fulfillment rises or falls.

The second development, the economic restructuring described by Wilson and others, also affected the entire nation, but it hit blacks especially hard. It appears to have slowed the increase in semi-skilled manufacturing jobs, which can provide stable employment at adequate wages to people without a college degree. The greater growth of the service sector benefited black women more than black men because many service jobs—secretaries, sales clerks, waitresses—had been labeled as women's work. The expansion of government social welfare programs may also have increased the economic independence of women from men. These changes in the labor market eroded the earning potential of black males, which in turn lessened their ability to support a wife and children.

The way that blacks responded to these broad-based cultural and economic shifts, I would argue, was conditioned by their history and culture—by what was on the spice rack. Faced with difficult times economically, many blacks responded by drawing upon a model of social support that was in their cultural repertoire, a way of making it from day to day passed down by African Americans who came before them. This response relied heavily on extended kinship networks and deemphasized marriage. It tapped a traditional source of strength in African American society: cooperation and sharing among a large network of kin. It was also consistent with the general movement away from marriage in the United States. Faced with a society-wide shift toward later and less stable marriages and with the declining job prospects for black men, black women didn't postpone childbearing, as whites did. Instead, they still started having children at the young ages typical of mothers of both races in the 1950s, even though most were not yet married. These young black mothers relied heavily on their own mothers and other kin to help care for their babies. For most, a marriage followed the birth of their first child by several years, and was not necessarily to that child's father. Had these adaptations not been part of African American culture, the retreat from marriage and the rise in the proportion of births to unmarried women probably would not have been as dramatic. The increased reliance on extended kin has allowed many poor blacks to have two or three children, pay their bills, and put food on the table—and obtain emotional support as well. But this family configuration also can have costs for parents and children.[76]

## Family Structure and Poverty

The health of the economy, not family structure, has been the main force affecting poverty among blacks over the last few decades. Poverty among blacks dropped dramatically during the economic boom of the 1960s. In 1959 more than half the black population was living below the official government poverty level; by 1969 the proportion was down to one-third. But little progress was made during the 1970s, as the economy slowed following the 1973 oil price shock. In the early 1980s poverty rates actually rose somewhat during the recession. The economist James P. Smith estimated that the black poverty rate in 1980 would have been 30 percent lower if blacks had the same proportion of female-headed households as whites.[77] A 30 percent reduction, although substantial, would still have left blacks much poorer than whites. Moreover, the recession of the early 1980s seemed to affect families without regard to the number of adults present; studies show that changes in household composition had little to do with the rise in poverty for blacks and whites.[78]

In addition, one can't assume that blacks fall into poverty only when they become part of a female-headed household. Mary Jo Bane examined the histories of persons in the PSID to determine the relationship between female-headed households and poverty. She found that about two-thirds of blacks who were poor after becoming part of a female-headed household had been poor beforehand. Much of the poverty among black female-headed households, Bane concludes, is really a "reshuffling" of the black poor from one kind of household to another. A majority of poor, unmarried black mothers were poor before they became mothers; becoming female family heads didn't cause their poverty.[79]

Many observers still argue, however, that living in a female-headed household makes it more difficult to climb out of poverty. Recall that female-headed households constitute a majority of households whose members are persistently poor year after year, whereas persons who are poor for a spell of only a year or two mainly live in households headed by a male. One of the themes of the voluminous writings in the 1980s about the "underclass" is the difficulty that low-income single mothers and their children have escaping from poverty. Several studies of national survey data by Sara McLanahan and her colleagues demonstrate that persons who grow up in such households are more likely to drop out of high school, have children while teenagers, or become single parents themselves.[80]

I think it is likely that the great increase in single-parent households among blacks has, in fact, retarded the movement of family members out of poverty. Consider again the extended family networks that by economic constraints and cultural preference are common among low-income blacks. To think of the households in such networks as separate "single-parent families" may be misleading. As we have seen, a single parent's family often consists of a number of kin spread over several households—a mother, an aunt, a brother, an in-law, and so forth, who share and exchange goods, services, and emotional support. In the late 1960s, anthropologist Carol Stack studied a low-income black neighborhood in the Midwest and found that most residents were part of a complex network of relatives and close friends who exchanged mutual support.[81] In effect, these kin networks helped to socialize the hardships of poverty and cushion its inevitable shocks.

Several scholars have argued that these extended kin networks are a rational, adaptive response by low-income blacks to their economic situation—perhaps the best response under the circumstances.[82] Moreover, network ties sometimes can be useful to the upwardly mobile. In a typical history, one large extended family in rural Mississippi saw many of its members move to Detroit, Chicago, and other northern cities in the 1950s and 1960s, where their standard of living improved.[83] The later migrants found jobs and places to live through relatives who had migrated earlier, much as white migrants to industrializing cities did 50 to 100 years earlier.[84] This extended family had many two-parent households, and its Mississippi members were active in the local churches and in the civil rights movement. The Northerners kept in touch, visited during vacations, and sometimes sent children or adults back to Mississippi to live. But they did not engage in day-to-day sharing of income and labor.

Despite its strengths, a kin network that shares resources can pose difficulties for its members. Group loyalty, the essence of the strength of the family networks, can conflict with the goals of individuals. For instance, it may be difficult for a single person or a couple to amass enough resources to advance their own standard of living because of their obligations to others in the network. Another, poorer extended family in the same Mississippi county owned no land and relied primarily on sharecropping. Some of its fourteen households specialized in raising livestock, others grew sweet and white potatoes, and some contributed labor for planting or harvesting. Each household shared its goods and services with the others. The exchanges were circular and were not immediately reciprocated: household A might give meat to household B, which might give vegetables to household C, which might at a later time give potatoes to household A. Few people were able to accumulate enough resources to leave this network because to do so they had to withhold their food and labor—which meant they could not call on their relatives for help. One woman described relatives who exchanged goods and services as "family members" and those that did not as merely "other kin"; the latter gave and received little assistance.

When a young woman in the Midwestern neighborhood studied by Stack wanted to marry, the members of her network discouraged her from doing so. Her contribution was valuable to the others, and they feared she would withdraw from the network if she married. As a matter of fact, during the study she did marry and, recognizing that the demands of the network might conflict with the demands of her marriage, that evening she left the state with her husband. In another instance an older couple unexpectedly inherited $1,500. At first they decided to use the money as a down payment on a house, but others in their network soon made a series of requests for money that couldn't be refused. Several relatives needed train fare to attend a funeral; another needed $25 so her phone wouldn't be turned off; a sister faced eviction because of overdue rent. The local welfare office also helped take the surplus away by cutting the couple's children off welfare temporarily. Within six weeks the windfall was gone.[85]

Stack's study suggests that it is difficult for anyone in these networks to raise his or her level of living until everyone in the network is able to raise his or her level. A person who marries or gets a job and wishes to move up the social ladder may be forced to leave the network; but this is a risky step, not to be taken lightly, given the high rate of marital dissolution and the insecure nature of low-wage work. Although the family networks among low-income blacks ease the burdens of poverty, they may also make it difficult for individuals to rise out of poverty.

Moreover, most of those who write about black family networks seem to assume that nearly all black single parents have strong, stable networks available to them. But studies suggest otherwise—especially in the poorest neighborhoods. Single parents in a very poor, crime-ridden black neighborhood in Philadelphia tended to isolate themselves and their children from the neighborhood, according to fieldwork by Frank F. Furstenberg, Jr., and his colleagues.[86] Many mothers either had few relatives living nearby or had weak ties to those who were near. Faced with limited help from kin and community, scared of losing their children to crime and drugs, parents withdrew into their apartments. They restricted their children's movements, accompanied them to the playground, scrutinized their friends, and in general devoted a great deal of time and effort to monitoring and supervising their behavior. As the authors note, this individualistic strategy of coping with the perils of daily life contrasts with the kin network strategy noted by Stack and others.

The extreme deprivation and danger in the poorest inner-city neighborhoods may overwhelm the capacity of kin networks to help. Among all black families with children, the share of income earned by the poorest fifth dropped in the 1970s and 1980s, whereas the share earned by the top fifth has grown—even more sharply than among whites.[87] Families at the bottom of the economic ladder are simply poorer than they used to be. With less to share, kin networks may provide less help.[88]

More fortunate families, in addition, often move out. In another black Philadelphia neighborhood, Furstenberg and his colleagues found that parents were losing confidence in the ability of schools, churches, and community groups to help them bring up their children. The primary response among working-class and middle-class families was to move to a better neighborhood. It is a strategy followed by working-class and middle-class blacks nationwide. Nearly as many African Americans, for example, lived in the suburbs of Washington, D.C., in

1980 as in the city itself.[89] It also is a self-reinforcing strategy: as better-off families leave a neighborhood, the community institutions deteriorate further, which encourages more out-migration. Increasingly, the single-parent families in inner-city ghetto neighborhoods are the ones left behind by the exodus of the better-off. Those who remain probably have fewer kin to turn to. They probably also have less education, are less likely to be literate, and are less adept at making use of the declining number of opportunities their communities offer themselves and their children.

Dennis P. Hogan, Lingxin Hao, and William L. Parish studied information about the kinship networks of young mothers in a 1984 national survey of young adults aged 19 to 26. They tabulated the proportion of mothers who were receiving at least one of the following forms of support: (1) they lived in an extended family (that is, with an adult relative other than their husband); or (2) they received half or more of their income from someone other than their husband; or (3) they received unpaid child care assistance. Sixty-eight percent of the black single mothers received at least one of these three forms of support compared to 54 percent of white single mothers—showing once again that blacks are more involved in kin networks.[90] But the glass also is one-third empty: 32 percent of the black mothers did not receive any of these forms of aid.

The researchers also found that the amount of support young mothers receive diminishes rapidly over time. About two-thirds of the 19-year-old black single mothers were living with their own mothers; the proportion dropped to about half among 21-year-old single mothers and to about one-third among 25-year-old single mothers. The decline in the proportion of black single mothers who received child care assistance from kin was similar but less steep, falling from about three-fourths of the 19-year-olds to a bit more than half of the 25-year-olds. Income support declined as well. So although most young black single mothers live with, or close to, kin and receive crucial support from them, much of this support is temporary. As the young mothers enter their twenties, they tend to move out of their parents' homes. What's more, their relatives may not be able to provide so much assistance; many of the grandmothers are in their thirties or forties and are themselves working full-time. Moreover, the mothers in the study who received support or were living near kin were not more likely to be employed or to work more hours at the time of the survey.[91] The researchers conclude that the amount of help young black mothers receive from kin is substantial but rather short-lived and that it is not enough to overcome the disadvantages of being a single parent.

It is true that single mothers who live with their own mothers or other kin appear to supervise their teenagers' behavior about as well as do mothers who live with their husbands.[92] But Hogan, Hao, and Parish's findings suggest that by the time their children are teenagers, most single mothers aren't living with their own mothers. And, as I noted above, many of the grandmothers are working themselves. A grandmother who works the evening shift at a local hospital probably won't be very helpful in supervising her teenage grandchildren's social life. Many young grandmothers experience grandmotherhood as what Linda Burton has called an "off-time" event. They love their grandchildren and help their daughters; but they aren't ready to consider themselves grandparents, and they are leading busy lives as workers and as parents themselves. A twenty-seven-year-old grandmother, who herself had a new baby, talked to Burton about the strain caused by the arrival of her new grandchild: "Everyone is pissed off at each other. No one wants to take responsibility for raising this baby. Not even my mother [the great-grandmother]; she's too busy doing her own thing . . . I'm so mad . . . But who do I have to talk to about the way *I* feel?"[93] Still, black grandparents selflessly provide great amounts of support to their daughters after the birth of a grandchild. By the time the grandchildren are teenagers, however, the grandparents may be providing much less direct help.

## Public Policy

What the response of public policy ought to be to the changes in African American families is a difficult and contentious issue. I have described how black families have adapted to changes in the labor market and to a society-wide cultural shift away from strong marital ties by relying increasingly on ties to a network of extended kin. These networks can provide a great deal of assistance; they constitute a family resource not found as frequently among whites. But this strategy has limits. The resources of the networks can be stretched too thin by deepening poverty. Not every poor person has a functioning network. The networks may discourage individuals from accumulating resources, marrying, and moving out of poverty. There is a case to be made, consequently, for creating policies that support stable, two-parent families—which, for the most part, are headed by a married couple. The justification is not that a marriage-based system is universally superior but rather that two-parent families are better able to amass resources and supervise their children in an industrialized society such as the United States. As Harriette Pipes McAdoo writes in an article about upward mobility among African Americans, "The earnings of two adults who are sharing parenting and financial support are needed for families to maintain their economic levels and to garner the resources to move on to higher statuses."[94]

Nonetheless we must accept that extended kin networks will remain the central family unit for many African Americans in the near future, even if economic conditions improve. African Americans have a cultural tradition of relying more heavily on extended families, and they live in a society in which marriage is everywhere on the decline. Although racial differences could lessen substantially, no feasible government policy will result in black families' approaching the two-parent ideal. Nor need this occur; despite their limitations, networks of single parents and their relatives often provide for and nurture their members as well as nuclear families could. In any case, it is inevitable that a large proportion of poor black children will grow up in single-parent households in the next decade or two.

There are, consequently, two worthy objectives for policies that aid poor black families: encouraging marriage among those who wish to do so and assisting single parents and their children in the remaining kin networks. The dilemma is that these two objectives can clash. For example, some have advocated slashing public assistance benefits as a way to push more poor people into marriage. If welfare benefits were cut in half, marriage, or at least cohabitation, probably would increase among the poor. But many of these unions would have a shaky economic foundation unless employment prospects for black males also increased. In all likelihood, most single mothers would either remain unmarried or enter unstable unions. Most would continue to rely on kin networks, whose resources would be reduced; and their children would suffer further reductions in an already low living standard.

It is also suggested by some that the government support the family by providing cash payments to parents. These payments could be accomplished by a refundable tax credit, by increasing the federal income tax exemption for dependent children or, in the style of European child allowances, through providing cash subsidies directly to the parents of all children.[95] A tax credit or child allowance program such as this would aid poor parents and children. But if all parents were eligible for assistance, regardless of their marital status, it would not necessarily encourage marriage. If payments were limited to married parents, it would discriminate against poor children from single-parent households. Moreover, such a marriage payment would have to be substantial to make much difference. The experience of European countries that have tried to promote births by offering cash subsidies is that large subsidies must be provided to bring about even a modest rise.[96]

The best way to encourage marriage without penalizing single-parent households would be to strengthen black men's connection to the labor force. I noted earlier the precipitous decline in earnings among young black men and the growing number who report no earnings at all. Earnings and employment are strong determinants, although not the only determinants, of marriage. One national study found that young black men who were employed full-time were twice as likely to marry in the next year as were those who had experienced some recent unemployment; the effects were much smaller among white men.[97] Black women's wages are lower than black men's wages, but this is due to their gender, not their race—the earnings of black and white women are roughly equal, on average. The challenge over the next generation is to find ways to achieve the kind of racial equality in the workplace for black men that the 1970s and 1980s brought to black women. It is a very difficult challenge to meet.

The second option for aiding the poor is to provide more assistance directly to single mothers and their children. These policies—whether through cash assistance or job training or reducing the wage gap between women and men—probably will discourage marriage somewhat by increasing the economic independence of single mothers and their children. But they also will raise the living standard of the large number of children who will remain in single-parent households. The 1988 Family Support Act changed the emphasis of welfare policy from cash assistance (such as the almost universally disliked Aid to Families with Dependent Children program[98]) to supported work—job training and placement with temporary day care assistance and medical coverage. It also strengthened the enforcement of child support payments by absent parents. The 1988 act is a tacit admission by both liberals and conservatives that marriage is not likely to be the solution to the poverty of most poor, single mothers and their children. The best that can be hoped for is that single mothers will be able to support themselves and their children without long-term reliance on public funds. Unless nonemployed black men are brought into the labor force in larger numbers, I think that the picture will remain the same. We ought to acknowledge that a major move to marriage among the poor is unlikely and set our social welfare policies accordingly.

Much of the heated debate about the black family centers on two competing assertions: that the increase in single-parent households has harmful consequences and that this increase represents an adaptive, resourceful response to poverty. I believe that to understand what happened to the black family over the past few decades, we must accept that *both* of these perspectives are true. The increased reliance on extended kin, and the de-emphasis on marriage, is an altruistic strategy that has allowed many poor mothers and children to survive by sharing what little they have with a broad network of relatives and friends. It is rooted in African American culture; nevertheless, it is a response chosen under duress. Low-income black families have opted to rely even more heavily on extended kin networks in recent decades not just because of a broad cultural shift but also because of the deteriorating earnings and employment of poorly educated black men. Consequently, just as we must resist condemning this response as pathological, we must not commit the opposite error of celebrating it.

To progress toward a more humane public policy we must end the battle between advocates of cultural and economic explanations. There is no contradiction in accepting both. The change in the black family is in part a response to changes in the labor market. But in addition, it is a way of coping that was culturally available; it was in the repertoire of responses to adversity that African Americans have passed down from generation to generation. When E. Franklin Frazier made "Granny: The Guardian of the Generations" a chapter title in his classic book on black families, he might have been writing about the black grandmothers we listened to at the senior citizens' center.[99] Describing her hands-on relationship with a fourteen-year-old grandson, one grandmother told us: "I'm going to tell you right now, he is no angel. You hear me? He calls me the worst grandmother in the world, the meanest one. Because this child doesn't have a father there with us, and I was raised in a family without the father's image. So that means I've got to be a little stronger, we've got to be very strong, with what's out there in this world now."[100] That grandmothers are this strong a presence in their grandchildren's lives should be admired. That people in tough circumstances figured out a way to survive should be applauded. But the contradictions and costs of their response should not be ignored.

# The State of Our Unions

On February 13, 1986, a reporter from the Stamford, Connecticut, *Advocate* called the sociologist Neil Bennett at Yale University. She told him she was writing a Valentine's Day article on love in Fairfield County, and she asked if he had any information on the state of marriage. Coincidently, Professor Bennett and his colleagues David Bloom at Harvard and Patricia Craig at Yale had recently estimated the likelihood that young women who remained single until their thirties would eventually marry. Bennett retrieved a draft of a working paper and read some figures to the reporter. If current marriage rates continued, he said, white, college-educated women who were still single at age 30 would have only a 20 percent chance of ever marrying; those who remained single until age 35 would have only a 5 percent chance; and at age 40 the chance would be a mere 1 percent.

Recognizing a good story, the reporter broadened the focus of her article, which ran on page one the next day with Bennett's projections featured. An Associated Press reporter read the story and sent a dispatch over the national wire. The next day the figures from Bennett's working paper were printed in newspapers across the country.

The reaction was spectacular. The Harvard-Yale Study, as it came to be known, struck a nerve among single women everywhere. It seemed to show that for young female professionals, marriage postponed too long was marriage forgone. It was discussed on talk shows, analyzed in opinion columns, and noted on the network news in a crescendo of public attention that peaked on June 2 when, in an apparent first for social science, a graph drawn from one of the tables in the working paper appeared on the cover of *Newsweek.* Its downward slope showed, in the memorable words of the author of the cover story, that a forty-year-old woman's probability of marrying was so low that she was "more likely to be killed by a terrorist."

In fact, Bennett, Bloom, and Craig later backed off from these projections, and a Census Bureau demographer reported substantially higher probabilities.[1] But what was notable about the incident was not the size of the numbers but the size of the reaction. It was surprising to find that, in a society in which sexual relations among unmarried adults are accepted and cohabiting unions are common, so many people cared. It is hard to imagine a similar study generating such a strong reaction in Sweden, where long-term cohabiting relationships are more frequent and nearly half of all children are born out of wedlock.[2] Despite the common (and correct) belief that marriage in the United States is a weakened institution, it is clear from the repercussions of the Harvard-Yale Study that the prospect of remaining unmarried until they were too old to have children made many women upset. All too aware of the ticking of the biological clock, single women in their thirties were distressed by the news that they might not marry before midnight. Their distress revealed the continuing strength among Americans, at least in the middle class, of the belief that it is preferable to raise children in a marriage.

And yet the young women who were so shaken by the study belonged to a generation that was postponing marriage to an extent not seen since the beginning of the century. The postponement had several causes, as noted in Chapter 2. Among them were the greater investment by young women in labor market skills and work experience, the greater acceptance of premarital sex, and the ability to avoid unwanted pregnancies and births through contraception and abortion. It was also the first generation in which cohabitation outside of marriage became widespread among the middle class, primarily as a short-term testing ground for marriage. It was a generation in which nearly one-fourth of all births occurred outside of wedlock. And it was a generation in which half or more of all first marriages were projected to end in divorce.

This paradox of a retreat from marriage amid continuing strong sentiment in favor of it needs to be addressed. Although marriage has declined as a cultural imperative and as an economic necessity, it continues to derive sentimental strength from its persistence as the preferred form of union, especially if children are involved.

## Marriage as a Cultural Imperative

In 1957, men in a national survey were asked, "Suppose that all you knew about a man was that he did not want to get married. What would you guess he was like?" Women in the survey were asked the same question about a hypothetical woman. Half the sample responded that the person probably was deficient in some way: sick, immoral, selfish, or neurotic. But when the same question was asked in a 1976 national survey, only one-third of the sample gave such negative opinions.

The two surveys also included the question "Thinking about a man's (woman's) life, how is a man's (woman's) life changed by being married?" In 1957, 40 percent of the sample responded positively, describing marriage as opening new opportunities and enlarging life. Just 20 percent expressed negative views, emphasizing burdens and restrictions. In contrast, almost as many people in the 1976 sample expressed negative views as positive views. The authors of a book about these surveys wrote, "Perhaps nowhere in the book will we see such a dramatic change from 1957 to 1976 as we have in men's and women's increased tolerance of people who reject marriage as a way of life."[3]

The two surveys are part of a series of studies conducted over the past three decades by social scientists at the Institute for Social Research at the University of Michigan. These studies have mapped changes in the beliefs of Americans about how people should live their family lives. In a review of the studies, Arland Thornton reported striking changes in attitudes during the 1960s and 1970s.[4] Americans' increasing tolerance of people who reject marriage was matched by greater tolerance of divorce, childlessness, and more egalitarian family roles for men and women.

For example, in 1962, only 51 percent of young adult women agreed with the statement "Divorce is usually the best solution when a couple can't seem to work out their marriage problems." When the same women were reinterviewed in 1977, 80 percent agreed with the statement. As for childlessness, 85 percent of the women, all of whom had recently given birth to children, answered positively in 1962 to the question "Do you feel almost all married couples who can *ought* to have children?" But just 43 percent answered positively to the same question when reinterviewed in 1980.

What occurred was, in Thornton's words, an "erosion of norms" about family life, a weakening of the cultural rules that guide behavior. Americans became more tolerant of alternatives to conventional patterns of marriage and childbearing. The erosion appeared to be part of a broader cultural shift toward an emphasis on autonomy and personal growth. Family life became a matter of personal choice in which individuals made decisions based on a calculus of self-interest and self-fulfillment.[5] Marriage was still desirable, but one no longer had to be married to be a proper member of adult society.

## Marriage as an Economic Necessity

The formation of marriage has not rested merely on cultural norms. Marriage, at least until recently, was an economic necessity. It was a partnership of a man and a woman who cooperated in order to produce the goods and services they both needed. To be economically viable, a married couple often needed to be part of a larger household economy. During the early decades of industrialization, adults, children, and other family members pooled income from wages into a household fund. In late-nineteenth-century America it was common for working-class households to take in boarders and lodgers to augment income.[6] Life outside a family context was precarious at best. It was necessary to rely on kin because of the absence of government support. Medicare, Aid to Families with Dependent Children, unemployment compensation— most of the apparatus of the welfare state emerged in the United States only after the Great Depression.

Even as recently as the end of World War II, incomes were low enough, and affordable housing was scarce enough, to discourage individuals from going it alone. In 1947, the median family income was equivalent to $17,689 when expressed in terms of 1990 purchasing power. Median family income doubled to $35,379 (in 1990 purchasing power) by 1973, largely because of rising productivity.[7] Millions of families moved into newly constructed single-family homes. In addition, rising incomes made it possible for individuals to live outside of a family setting, and many did. The proportion of households containing just one person rose from 7 percent in 1940 to 17 percent in 1970.[8]

By the 1970s, marriage was much less of an economic necessity, especially to women. It was not merely more acceptable to be unmarried and living on one's own, it was much more feasible. Although women's wages had stayed low relative to men's, their wages had risen in absolute terms. And the ceaseless surge of married women into the labor force had opened opportunities and made working outside the home an accepted, even expected, social role. As noted in Chapter 3, it is still difficult for many divorced mothers to support themselves and their children on modest wages and intermittent child support payments. But it *is* possible, and that possibility allows more unhappy husbands to leave their wives and more unhappy wives to leave their husbands.

This story of rising incomes may not jibe with the common argument that married women have been pushed into the labor market—that they are working because they have to, rather than because they choose to. But the "have to" argument is mainly applicable to the period since 1973. After the oil price shock of 1973, wages entered a period of stagnation and decline that continued through the 1980s. In 1984 median family income was $33,162 (in 1990 dollars), a decline of 6 percent since 1973. The decline would have been even larger had not the increase in wives' employment compensated for the lower wages of their husbands.[9] Also, part of the increase in wives' employment, both before and after 1973, was a result of rising consumer aspirations. The line between "have to" and "choose to" becomes blurred when everyone else on your block has a second car and a VCR.[10]

## Marriage as a Persistent Preference

Given the decline of marriage as a cultural imperative and an economic necessity, one may wonder why the institution persists. The first answer is that there is still some social pressure to marry and some economic gains associated with marrying. The pressure and gains are more pronounced when children—or the prospect of having children—is involved. Only 30 percent of the never-married persons under age 35 in the 1987–88 National Survey of Families and Households agreed with the statement "It would be all right for me to have children without being married if I had definite plans to marry the father/mother."[11] As was noted in Chapter 3, the economic situation of single mothers and their children is often precarious; it is economically advantageous for mothers to be married.

More important, marriage is still a much sought-after status, still the culturally preferred way to form long-term heterosexual unions. To be sure, it is no longer seen as the only proper status for adults; being single or, to some extent, cohabiting is acceptable. But for most people being married is preferable. Even with the pronounced changes in marriage behavior since the 1960s, all but a small minority of young adults still expect to marry. Among high school seniors in 1980, for example, 10 percent of men and 5 percent of women did not expect to marry, which was only a modest increase over the 8 percent and 3 percent, respectively, who did not expect to marry in a comparable 1960 survey.[12] When high school seniors in 1985 and 1986 were asked how important to them was "having a good marriage and family life," 93 percent of the women and 86 percent of the men responded that it was "extremely important" or "quite important."[13] In the 1985 and 1986 surveys, conducted at a time when half or more of all marriages were projected to end in divorce, 66 percent of all women and 55 percent of all men responded that if they did get married it was "very likely" that they "would stay married to the same person for life" and another 21 and 26 percent, respectively, responded that is was "fairly likely."

In Chapter 1 I noted that the average duration of a cohabiting union is only about one-and-one-half years; most couples either marry or break up in fairly short order. Furthermore, marriage is still seen as sexually exclusive by a large majority of adults. The General Social Survey, a national sample of adults conducted in most years since 1973, has included the question "What is your opinion about a *married* person having sexual relations with someone *other* than the marriage partner—is it always wrong, almost always wrong, wrong only some-times, or not wrong at all?" Some earlier data, reported by Thornton, suggest that attitudes became more permissive between 1965 and the start of the GSS. But since 1973, the proportion responding "always wrong" has increased among men and women under 30 and stayed constant among men and women 30 or older. In 1985 the proportion ranged from 67 percent among men under 30 to 79 percent among women 30 or older.[14]

So the institution of marriage is tenacious, even though it has been weakened by recent developments. Fidelity, stability, and security in the context of a legally recognized marriage constitute a highly valued kind of relationship. Moreover, as the attitude data reviewed here show, women place a higher value on this kind of relationship than do men. The difference likely reflects the greater role of women in childrearing, a set of tasks that is more easily carried out within a marriage, and the greater economic gains to women from marrying. Nevertheless, men also show substantial attachment to marriage.

The paradox is that when Americans finally enter a marriage, they judge it increasingly by a single standard—personal fulfillment—that is difficult to maintain. In one recent study, the authors found that many married couples had difficulty even finding "a language in which to articulate their reasons for commitments that went beyond the self."[15] Judgments about the level of personal fulfillment are subject to continual revision. With few normative, economic, or structural constraints on breaking up, a negative judgment is more likely to lead to a divorce. Indeed, with personal fulfillment accepted as such a predominant indicator of marital health, it is difficult for unhappy individuals to remain married. Fifty years ago, even thirty, unhappy couples hesitated to divorce; now they are almost compelled to.

## Marriage and Public Policy

Is there cause for concern about these changes in how we think about marriage and how we live our family lives? Certainly one's personal answer to this question can vary greatly depending on one's moral beliefs. Some Americans find the changes to be antithetical to their values; many others, as we have seen, tolerate and accept them; still others welcome them. Judgments about the moral fitness of various forms of family life are outside the boundaries of a social-scientific work such as this. But there are some objectives of family life that society has a collective interest in supporting. Foremost among them is the adequate rearing of the next generation.

What has occurred since the mid-1960s is a weakening of the link between marriage and the care of children. The facts have been laid out in the previous chapters. The question here is whether we, as a society, should take steps to strengthen the link in order to improve the well-being of children. If the encouragement of marriage were to become a goal of public policy, three propositions would have to be demonstrated: first, that children who live with married parents are substantially better off than are those who do not; second, that marriage itself—rather than some associated or preexisting factor—causes the observed differences in children's well-being; and third, that there is a reasonable prospect that public policies could increase the number and stability of marriages without an unacceptable loss of personal freedom.

The first proposition—that children who live with married parents are better off—is easily demonstrated, especially with respect to income. According to data from the 1980 census, 9 percent of children who were living with two married parents had family incomes below the poverty level, compared to 18 percent of children living with cohabiting parents and 47 percent of those living only with their mother.[16] There are also differences in non-economic outcomes, as noted in Chapters 3 and 4. To cite one additional example, a study conducted in Baltimore by Frank F. Furstenberg, Jr., and his colleagues followed the children of black unwed mothers through age seventeen. The odds that a child had repeated a grade in school more than doubled if the mother was not married at the seventeen-year follow-up.[17] In addition, recent research shows that women who grow up in single-parent families are themselves more likely to have children before marrying and to see their own marriages break up.[18] The studies reviewed in Chapter 3 suggested that children whose parents divorce appear, on average, to have moderately higher levels of emotional problems than do children whose parents remained married, although some of these problems arise before the break-up.

The second proposition—that marriage or its absence is the cause of these differences—is more difficult to substantiate. The problem is to determine whether living with married parents makes children better off or whether children who would be better off anyway for other reasons are the ones whose parents get married and stay married. Consider the relationship between the growth of single-parent households headed by women and trends in poverty among women and children. In much public commentary, the growth of so-called female-headed households is associated with increases in poverty.[19] An analysis of the longitudinal Panel Study of Income Dynamics (PSID), however, showed that, particularly among blacks, many poor, female household heads were poor *before* they split off to form their own households. Among black women who formed female-headed households that had incomes below the poverty line, 62 percent had lived in households with incomes below the poverty line before they formed their own households; among white women the comparable figure was 24 percent.[20]

An analysis of remarriages among women in the PSID showed a similar kind of selectivity at work. The authors first noted that women who remarried following a divorce recouped much of the loss of family income that their divorce brought about. But they also presented evidence that the divorced women who remained unmarried would not have gained nearly as much income from a new husband had they chosen to remarry. In others words, those who had the most to gain economically had already remarried; were the others to do so the benefits to them and their children would be less.[21]

Still, the PSID data clearly show that events such as a divorce often affect children's economic well-being adversely. In most families, children remain with their mothers after a parental divorce; the standard of living of women and children in the PSID dropped by about 30 percent in the first year following a divorce.[22] The studies of the emotional effects of divorce also suggest that sometimes the separation and its aftermath do cause difficulties for children. The lesson I draw from all of these studies is that decisions about marriage and divorce are sometimes the cause and sometimes the result of the well-being of parents and children. Proposition two is true often enough to justify concern about the rising number of single-parent households.

I am skeptical, however, of the validity of the third proposition—that feasible public policies could be created to encourage and support marriage. There are, I think, stringent limits on what public policy can do to support marriage. Much of the decrease in marriage is due to the aforementioned declines in the cultural imperative to marry and in the economic need to marry. To increase marriage, one of these declines would have to be reversed. Strengthening the cultural imperative would take a massive shift in public attitudes toward marriage and, more generally, about the obligations and responsibilities individuals have toward others. Americans would have to value more highly the satisfactions in life that can come from commitment to others and devalue the satisfactions that come from self-fulfillment. Such a sea change is possible, although at the present time I think it unlikely.

More important, it is hard to see how government policy alone could produce such a change. The home-and-family-centered values of the 1950s were produced mainly by the hardship of the depression and the war, the small birth cohorts of the 1930s, and the postwar economic boom—not by government policies. Nor did the policies of the 1960s and 1970s produce the continual increase in women's labor force participation, the birth control pill, the OPEC oil price shock, or the human potential movement. To reverse the drift away from marriage would require events of this magnitude—another depression or a large-scale religious revival—not merely a revision of the tax code. Although government surely could play a role in supporting a change in values, it could not create the change itself.

In the early 1990s, there are a set of public policies labeled as "pro-family" that are gaining widespread, bipartisan support. These include tougher enforcement of court-ordered child support payments by non-custodial parents and larger tax credits or exemptions for families with children. Advocates of larger tax exemptions, for example, note that the value of the federal exemption for dependents has been severely eroded by inflation over the past few decades, leaving families with a heavier tax burden. The proposed remedies, increasing the exemption or replacing it with a refundable tax credit, certainly would provide more money to families with children—as would increased child support payments.[23] However, they wouldn't necessarily strengthen marriage because they would be available to single parents as well. Husbands and wives might reduce conflict in their marriages by using the extra money for childrearing expenses or to pay off debts. But spouses might also realize that the extra money would ease the financial strain on the custodial parent if they split up. Yet restricting tax benefits to married parents would discriminate against needy children in single-parent families. Similarly, better child support enforcement might dissuade some fathers from leaving their wives and children, but it also would provide a more reliable source of income for a mother who wished to end her marriage.

In order to create a truly pro-marriage policy, the government would have to make men and women dependent on each other by constraining behavior in ways few people would accept. For instance, a law that restricted women's employment opportunities probably would increase marital stability. Most Americans would oppose it, however, on egalitarian grounds (women should have the same opportunities as men), libertarian grounds (the government shouldn't constrain individual choices), economic grounds (women are an increasingly important part of the labor force), or all three. Limiting people's choices about family life would cut too deeply into the individual autonomy Americans value so highly.

My guess is that policies such as increased tax exemptions for dependents and stronger child support enforcement won't affect marriage rates much one way or the other. But I strongly favor such policies for a different reason: they undoubtedly would increase the well-being of children. They may not be pro-marriage but they certainly are pro-child. Children, through no actions of their own, have been caught up in the tidal wave of family change. They do not choose divorce for their parents; they do not choose to be born to teenagers. Public policy, reflecting our common concern about the rearing of the next generation, ought to provide more support to them. If some parents spend their increased incomes in ways that bolster their marriages, so much the better. But we should focus on the substantial help government can easily provide to children rather than on the unlikely prospect that government can influence the course of their parents' marriages.

Some observers claim that current programs that transfer income to the poor create disincentives to marry and to stay married. They argue that Aid to Families with Dependent Children (AFDC) and related transfer programs are responsible for much of the growth of single-parent families.[24] Those sympathetic to this view advocate that public assistance benefits be reduced sharply in order to force the poor to rely on spouses and the labor market. It is likely that increases in AFDC and related programs did account for some of the increase in female-headed households prior to 1980—by one estimate, between 9 and 14 percent of the increase between 1955 and 1975.[25] But since the late 1970s, public assistance benefits have, in fact, declined in purchasing power without any slackening of the growth of female-headed families.[26]

## Loss of Commonality

Chapter 4 examined the thesis of William J. Wilson and his associates, who have argued that the decline of marriage among African Americans is due to increasing male joblessness.[27] The implication is that young black women, as a result of the growing shortage of black men who can be expected to support a family, have turned away from marriage. If Wilson is correct, then public efforts to increase the proportion of black men who are employed could result in more marriages and fewer single-parent families. How to reduce unemployment among black males is without doubt a difficult question for policy makers. Wilson advocates a combination of macroeconomic policies to promote growth and tight labor markets, and on-the-job training and apprenticeships for the disadvantaged. Still, as I argued in Chapter 4, declining male employment probably cannot account directly for most of the recent drop in marriage among blacks.

In fact, the marriage patterns of blacks and whites have diverged over the past few decades. It is probably the case that marriage always has been less central to the family lives of African Americans than of white Americans. As noted in Chapter 4, a greater reliance on extended kin networks has been historically characteristic of blacks. But the differences in marriage have widened over the past few decades (as have differences in the age of mother at childbirth). In Chapter 4 I cited estimates by Thomas Espenshade that at the demographic rates prevalent in the latter half of the 1970s—rates that did not change much during the 1980s—the average black woman could expect to spend just 22 percent of her life in a marriage, whereas the average white woman could expect to spend virtually twice as long, 43 percent. Espenshade calculated that the gap in the late 1950s was smaller: 42 percent for black women compared to 54 percent for white women.[28] It is true that white family patterns have moved in the same direction: more postponement of marriage, a greater proportion of births born out of wedlock, more marital instability, and a greater reliance by women on kin networks. But with regard to the role of marriage, the two groups are farther apart now than they have been in the twentieth century. And the differences are not just a function of the behavior of the poor. Among college graduates who married for the first time in the 1970s, 21 percent of all black women already had given birth to a child. The comparable figure for non-Hispanic white women was 2 percent.[29]

Nevertheless, there also has been a growing stratification of family patterns within African American society. For example, differences in rates of separation and divorce among blacks according to education were relatively modest in 1960 but became larger by 1980.[30] The growing differences reflect the emergence since 1960 of a substantial black middle class whose family lives differ from both the white middle class and the black lower class. Among whites, the stratification of family patterns according to education does not appear to have changed much since 1960.

Enough has been written earlier in this book to suggest the limitations that family patterns of lower-class blacks may place on moving out of poverty. These patterns may also be viewed as adaptive—or at the least not maladaptive—strategies for dealing with the hardships of poverty.[31] Nevertheless, one may wonder whether black Americans are moving purposefully toward an adaptive family system that makes a radical break between marriage and childrearing or whether they, like white Americans, may be drifting toward new territory without much consideration of what the land will look like. And one may lament the loss of commonality between two racial groups that already have enough difficulty finding common ground.

## For Better or Worse

In 1985 evaluations of the state of marriage and the family were published by two leading sociological theorists, Randall Collins and Kingsley Davis.[32] What they had to say was so contradictory that one might think that they were talking about different societies.

"One conclusion that we are beginning to understand," writes Collins at the end of the first edition of his 509-page textbook on marriage and the family, "is that the family is not fundamentally weakening under all this change. In some respects it is even stronger than before." In past times, he tells his student readers, individuals had to remain in families because of economic need and patriarchal authority. But today, with rising affluence and declining male authority, "Love has become more important, not less. People make their marriages more for love." Collins acknowledges that "love is volatile" and that "people are less willing to stay in a marriage without love." Moreover, couples in dual-career marriages "will face the problem of fitting each partner's occupational priorities with their family life." He concludes the book: "No doubt this will keep marriages rather fluid, and the divorce rate (but also the remarriage rate) will remain fairly high. But during the times when each person is part of a family, the prevalent tone should be one of love. Although it lives with strains, nevertheless the family seems to be in better shape than ever."

Never mind that about half of the rather fluid marriages in the United States are projected to end in separation or divorce, that women and children's standard of living often plummets after divorce, that about 40 percent of all children will witness the break-up of their parents' marriages and perhaps 15 percent will witness divorce twice, that nearly half of all black children under age six are living with a mother who has never married, that about one-fourth of all children are born out of wedlock, that half of the approximately 463,000 teenagers who bore children in 1988 were both poor and unmarried—and that a small article on love in Fairfield County can strike terror in the hearts of a generation of college-educated women.[33]

Collins's panglossian view is the result of a misguided effort, common among liberal observers, to minimize the costs of recent family trends. One gingerly steps around divorce, out-of-wedlock childbearing, and childhood poverty and instead accentuates the positive. And there *are* positives: Americans value the increased personal autonomy that they have achieved in their private lives; although this achievement is easy to criticize, few critics would volunteer to be the first to forswear their own autonomy. Moreover, the changes in women's work and family roles over the past few decades have given American women broader opportunities and much greater control of their own lives. It is above all the wish to avoid sounding like an antifeminist, I think, that causes liberals to downplay the costs of the recent trends. And yet the true feminist position on all the changes is not obvious; recall that the big losers in the movement toward no-fault divorce have been middle-class mothers and children.

Davis, on the other hand, cannot be accused of optimism. Near the end of the introductory essay in his edited volume on marriage, he writes: "The general direction of the changes in marriage that the present book documents during the last forty years is toward a weakening of marriage as an institution. If this goes far enough, and if no satisfactory substitute for marriage emerges, industrial societies will not survive. In fact they are not replacing themselves now, in either number or quality of the next generation. The nonindustrial two-thirds of the world, ill equipped to provide adequate education, is producing 92 percent of the world's next generation. There is thus no assurance that industrial societies, as we have known them, will survive."

Whereas liberal defenders of family change focus on the emotionally enhanced relationships between adults and on the increased autonomy of women, conservatives focus on instability and on children—in Davis's case, on the lack of children in sufficient "number or quality." Concern about population decline has been the major force behind family welfare legislation in many European countries for decades.[34] Davis is one of the few to raise the issue so far in the United States, but the chorus may grow louder in the 1990s.[35]

Without doubt, there are some valid issues about low birth rates that need to be discussed: How will a relatively smaller work force pay for social security and health care benefits for a large elderly population? With fewer children and more women at work, will the elderly be able to rely on support from their families, as many do today? Will there be a lack of dynamism in a population that isn't growing? Will opportunities for advancement be limited? Will the pace of technological innovation slow? But the end of industrial societies, as we have known them, is not in sight. Between 1950 and 1985, as western values spread throughout the developing world, the West's share of total population declined, according to one estimate, from 21 to 15 percent. A projected decline to about 9 percent forty years hence is unlikely to make much difference.[36] Moreover the 1980s saw an increase in the birth rates of women over age 30, at least in the United States.

Nor is the end of the family's ability to adapt at hand. Similar expressions of concern have been put forth for decades. Consider this warning, written by an expert on the family during the low-fertility years of the Great Depression: "The family is not indefinitely adaptable to modern society. . . . Only two logical alternatives appear feasible for governments wishing to induce births. They can go back to a rural-stable regime, or they can invent a new system of reproductive institutions."[37] The expert was none other than Kingsley Davis, writing in 1937 at the beginning of his career. His fears proved groundless. It turned out later that the family had not yet reached the limit of its ability to adapt and that governments did not have to invent a new system of reproductive institutions. What Davis did not and could not foresee was the great postwar baby boom.

This is not to say that we should expect another baby boom, nor that the family is infinitely malleable and resilient. The point is rather that the family has shown an ability to adjust to changing circumstances that is often underestimated. The problems of contemporary marriage are real and should not be minimized, but they do not suggest that the institution is fatally wounded. Nevertheless, even those who would applaud the gains in autonomy and opportunity for women and in a greater emphasis on love and companionship must acknowledge that the benefits have been achieved at a substantial cost. The cost includes more marital instability. Adults are freer to end unhappy marriages but do so through a process that is often emotionally and economically draining for parents and traumatic for children. The cost includes a greater proportion of children being born out-of-wedlock to single parents, some of whom have insufficient resources with which to raise their children. The costs include a greater risk of never marrying, a life trajectory that most Americans don't want but more are heading for. And the cost includes the possibility of never having children and therefore missing one of the primal satisfactions of the species.

The reason the Harvard-Yale Study caused an uproar was that it plainly laid out the personal costs of greater autonomy. That it suggested the costs might be greater for women than for men made it seem sexist. But it was only a description, a mirror held up to young adults. Although its estimates of lifelong singlehood proved overstated, the basic point—that there are costs of postponing marriage—was valid. Yet the acknowledgment of these costs does not imply an endorsement of the "traditional" family. A return to the time when married women rarely worked outside the home and economic constraints kept couples together is neither likely nor desirable. A much better response is to modify the other institutions of daily life in order to minimize the costs of family change. This is the thrust of proposals to alter the conditions of work—as by mandating leaves for the parents of infants and by improving access to affordable, quality child care—in order to make employment more compatible with family responsibilities. It is also the aim of recent and proposed laws to enforce the payment of child support obligations. Proposals such as these were gaining broad support at the beginning of the 1990s. I believe, and hope, that the 1990s will be a decade in which American society will finally make the adjustments necessary to minimize the costs of the changes in marriage and the family that have occurred in the last half of the twentieth century.

Notes

Index

# Notes

## Introduction

1. Quoted in Herman Lantz, Martin Schultz, and Mary O'Hara, "The Changing American Family from the Preindustrial to the Industrial Period: A Final Report," *American Sociological Review* 42 (June 1977): 406–421, at p. 413.
2. See, for example, Mary Jo Bane, *Here to Stay: American Families in the Twentieth Century* (New York: Basic Books, 1976).

## 1. Demographic Trends

1. Norman B. Ryder, "The Family in Developed Countries," *Scientific American* 231 (Sept. 1974): 122–132.
2. U.S. Bureau of the Census, *Historical Statistics of the United States, Colonial Times to 1970,* bicentennial ed., pt. 1 (Washington: U.S. Government Printing Office, 1975), p. 49.
3. Another trend in the timing of marriage is that the percentages never-married for men aged 20 to 24 have become more similar over time to those for women in the same age group. This reflects the lessening of the age gap between spouses in the twentieth century. Among people born in 1900 to 1904, the median age of men at first marriage was about four years more than the median age among women. By the time the depression cohort came of age, this difference had been reduced: for those born between 1930 and 1934, the difference was less than three years. The recent narrowing of the gap between the percent never-married among 20-to-24-year-old men and women suggests that the difference may still be declining. See U.S. Bureau of the Census, Current Population Reports, series P-20, no. 297, "Number, Timing, and Duration of Marriages and Divorces in the United States: June 1975" (Washington: U.S. Government Printing Office, 1976).
4. Kingsley Davis, "The American Family in Relation to Demographic Change," in Charles F. Westoff and Robert Parke, Jr., eds., Commission on Population Growth and the American Future, Research Reports, vol. 1, *Demographic and Social Aspects of Population Growth* (Washington: U.S. Government Printing Office, 1972), pp. 236–265.
5. Ibid.

6. Robert Schoen estimates that, were 1983 rates of marriage to continue, 88.3 percent of women would eventually marry. See "The Continuing Retreat from Marriage: Figures from 1983 Marital Status Life Tables," *Social Science Research* 71 (January 1987): 108–109. Two other papers present estimates separately for whites and blacks that, if combined into a single, weighted estimate, would imply that the overall percentage ever-marrying for women would be about 88 or 89. See Willard L. Rodgers and Arland Thornton, "Changing Patterns of First Marriage in the United States," *Demography* 22 (May 1985): 265–279; and Neil G. Bennett, David E. Bloom, and Patricia H. Craig, "The Divergence of Black and White Marriage Patterns," *American Journal of Sociology* 95 (November 1989): 692–722.

7. Before 1970 in France, consensual unions *(unions libres)* among the lower classes were the most common form of cohabitation. As in the United States, only after 1970 did cohabitation among other social classes become common. See Catherine Villeneuve-Gokalp, "Du mariage aux unions sans papiers: histoire récente des transformations conjugales," *Population* 45 (March-April 1990): 265–298. Similarly, Jan M. Hoem found that cohabitation was pioneered by the working class in Sweden; see "The Impact of Education on Modern Family-Union Formation," *European Journal of Population* 2 (1986): 113–133. On the relationship between formal marriage ceremonies and social class in developing countries, see Andrew Cherlin and Apichat Chamratrithirong, "Variations in Marriage Patterns in Central Thailand," *Demography* 25 (August 1988): 337–353.

8. Larry L. Bumpass and James A. Sweet, "National Estimates of Cohabitation," *Demography* (November 1989): 615–625.

9. Bumpass and Sweet, in "National Estimates," report that 50 percent of persons who were 30 to 34 at the time of the NSFH (1987–88) had already cohabited.

10. Ibid.

11. Larry L. Bumpass, James A. Sweet, and Andrew Cherlin, "The Role of Cohabitation in Declining Rates of Marriage," *Journal of Marriage and the Family* 53 (November 1991): 913–927.

12. Ibiathaj Arafat and Betty Yorburg, "On Living Together without Marriage," *Journal of Sex Research* 9 (May 1973): 97–106.

13. See Bumpass and Sweet, "National Estimates," and Robert J. Willis and Robert T. Michael, "Innovation in Family Formation: Evidence on Cohabitation in the 1986 Follow-Up Survey of the NLS/72 Sample," paper presented at the annual meeting of the Population Association of America, New Orleans, April 1988.

14. Bumpass and Sweet, "National Estimates."

15. Bumpass, Sweet, and Cherlin, "The Role of Cohabitation."

16. This perspective on cohabitation is advanced by Ronald R. Rindfuss and Audrey VandenHeuvel, "Cohabitation: An Alternative to Marriage or a Precursor to Being Single?" *Population and Development Review* 16 (December 1990): 703–726; and Robert Schoen and Dawn Owens, "A Further Look at First Unions and First Marriages," paper presented at the conference "Demographic Perspectives on the American Family: Patterns and Prospects," State University of New York at Albany, April 1990.

17. Bumpass, Sweet, and Cherlin, "The Role of Cohabitation."

18. For example, Eleanor D. Macklin, "Nonmarital Heterosexual Cohabitation," *Marriage and Family Review* 1 (March-April 1978): 1–12.

19. Bumpass and Sweet, "National Estimates." See also Alan Booth and David Johnson, "Premarital Cohabitation and Marital Success," *Journal of Family Issues* 9 (June 1988): 255–272; for Canada, T. R. Balakrishnan, K. Vaninadha Rao, Evelyne Lapierre-Adamcyk, and Karol J. Krotki, "A Hazard Model Analysis of the Covariates of Marriage Dissolution in Canada," *Demography* 24 (August 1987): 395–406; for Sweden, Neil G. Bennett, Ann Klimas Blanc, and David E. Bloom, "Commitment and the Modern Union: Assessing the Link between Premarital Cohabitation and Subsequent Marital Stability," *American Sociological Review* 53 (February 1988): 127–138. Henri Leridon, however, finds only a weak relationship in a 1985 French survey; see "Cohabitation, Marriage, Separation: An Analysis of Life Histories of French Cohorts from 1968 to 1985," *Population Studies* 44 (March 1990): 127–144. The various effects of legal status on the dissolutions of unions are explored in Jay D. Teachman, Jeffrey Thomas, and Kathleen Paasch, "Legal Status and the Stability of Coresidential Unions," *Demography* 26 (November 1991): 571–586.

20. Britta Hoem and Jan M. Hoem, "The Swedish Family: Aspects of Contemporary Developments," *Journal of Family Issues* 9 (September 1988): 397–424.

21. Ibid.; and Bumpass and Sweet, "National Estimates."

22. Andrew J. Cherlin, "The Weakening Link between Marriage and the Care of Children," *Family Planning Perspectives* 20 (November-December 1988): 302–306.

23. Louis Roussel, "L'évolution récente de la structure des ménages dans quelques pays industriels," *Population* 41 (November-December 1986): 913–934.

24. Ibid.

25. Henri Leridon and Catherine Villeneuve-Gokalp, "The New Couples:

Number, Characteristics, and Attitudes," *Population* 44, English Selection no. 1 (September 1989): 203–235.

26. Hoem and Hoem, "The Swedish Family"; Jan Trost, "Dissolution of Cohabitation and Marriage in Sweden," *Journal of Divorce* 2 (Summer 1979): 415–421; and Michel Bozon and François Héran, "La découverte du conjoint, II: Les scènes de rencontre dans l'espace social," *Population* 43 (January-February 1988): 121–150.

27. Norman B. Ryder, "Components of Temporal Variations in American Fertility," pp. 15–54 in Robert W. Hiorns, ed., *Demographic Patterns in Developed Societies* (London: Taylor and Francis, 1980).

28. Evans projected future experience by assuming that the pattern that cohorts show when the women are in their twenties (for example, high birth rates in their teenage years compared to low birth rates after age 20) reflect the likely level of fertility later in their reproductive years.

29. It was 3.0 for all women (white and nonwhite combined) born in 1891, 4.1 for the 1867 cohort, and perhaps 7 or 8 for those born in the early 1800s. See Ryder, "Components of Temporal Variations."

30. M. D. R. Evans, "American Fertility Patterns: A Comparison of White and Nonwhite Cohorts Born 1903–1956," *Population and Development Review* 12 (June 1986): 267–293.

31. Between 1980 and 1988, age-specific birth rates increased 36 percent for women aged 30–34 and 26 percent for women aged 35–39; see U.S. Bureau of the Census, "Fertility of American Women: June 1988," *Current Population Reports,* Series P-20, no. 436 (Washington: U.S. Government Printing Office, 1989).

32. Ibid.

33. Ibid.

34. The estimates for 1867 to 1949 are taken from Samuel H. Preston and John McDonald, "The Incidence of Divorce within Cohorts of American Marriages Contracted since the Civil War," *Demography* 16 (Feb. 1979): 1–25; the estimates are based on vital registration and census data. Preston and McDonald estimated the lifetime proportions divorcing for marriages surviving to 1970 by assuming that 1969 divorce and death rates will continue to hold in the future. The data for the 1950 to 1985 cohorts are taken from projections by James Weed, "U. S. Duration of Marriage Tables: A 1985 Update," paper presented at the annual meeting of the Southern Demographic Association, San Antonio, October 1988. Weed's projections are based on the actual experiences of these cohorts through 1985; he assumes that the divorce and death rates of the 1985 period will continue to hold in the future. There is one exception: for his earliest six cohorts,

1950 to 1955, he based projections on 1977 rates. See U.S. National Center for Health Statistics, Vital and Health Statistics, Series 3, no. 19, "National Estimates of Dissolution and Survivorship" (Washington: U.S. Government Printing Office, 1980). Thus, there is a slight discontinuity between 1955 and 1956. Another slight discontinuity is introduced by changing in 1950 from Preston and McDonald's estimate to Weed's more up-to-date projections. I have smoothed the data by plotting three-year moving averages in 1949, 1950, 1955, and 1956.

35. The solid curve in Figure 1-6 is the result of fitting a third-degree polynomial on time to the projected proportions by ordinary least squares regression. A similar procedure for 1867 to 1964 can be found in Preston and McDonald, "The Incidence of Divorce." The fitted values account for 99 percent of the variance in the projected proportions. The regression equation is:

$$ln\ p = -2.865 + .02068T + .00003137T^2 - .000000339T^3\ (R^2 = .992)$$

where $p$ is the predicted proportion divorcing, $T$ is year minus 1867, and $ln$ is the natural logarithm.

36. Weed, "U.S. Duration of Marriage Tables."

37. Robert Schoen, "The Continuing Retreat from Marriage: Figures from 1983 U.S. Marital Status Life Tables," Social Science Research 71 (January 1987): 108–109. Schoen and Weed both relied heavily on information on divorce collected by the U.S. National Center for Health Statistics. But their models differed somewhat: Weed estimated duration-specific probabilities of divorce for marriages, whereas Schoen estimated age-specific probabilities of divorce for individuals. Neither could include separation as an outcome since NCHS does not collect data on separations.

38. Teresa Castro Martin and Larry L. Bumpass, "Recent Trends in Marital Disruption," Demography 26 (February 1989): 37–51. Martin and Bumpass use retrospective marital histories collected as part of the June 1985 Current Population Survey by the Bureau of the Census. They adjusted the divorce figures upward to account for what they believe to be underreporting of separation and divorce in Bureau of the Census surveys. It is this upward adjustment, along with the inclusion of separation as an outcome, that makes their estimate so high.

39. Davis, "American Family"; see also Mary Jo Bane, Here to Stay: American Families in the Twentieth Century (New York: Basic Books, 1976).

40. In the first edition of this book, I calculated a rate of 40.5 in 1978. This was probably the peak or close to it. The total dissolution rate for marriages in a given year is the sum of the rates of dissolution by death and by divorce. Kingsley Davis calculated the total dissolution rate per 1,000

existing marriages for five-year intervals between 1860 and 1970. See Kingsley Davis, "The American Family in Relation to Demographic Change," in Charles F. Westoff and Robert Parke, Jr., *Demographic and Social Aspects of Population Growth*, Commission on Population Growth and the American Future, Research Reports, vol. 1 (Washington: U.S. Government Printing Office, 1972), Table 8. In order to calculate the rate for the latest available year, one needs three pieces of information: the number of existing marriages, the number of divorces, and the number of deaths of married persons. The first two are readily available. For 1989 the number of existing marriages was obtained from U.S. Bureau of the Census, Current Population Reports, series P-20, no. 445, "Marital Status and Living Arrangements: March 1989" (Washington: U.S. Government Printing Office, 1990). In order to be consistent with Davis's calculation, I took the number of married men (spouse present and spouse absent) as the indicator of the number of existing marriages. The number of divorces in 1989 is reported in U.S. National Center for Health Statistics, Monthly Vital Statistics Report, vol. 38, no. 13, *Annual Summary of Births, Marriages, Divorces, and Deaths: United States, 1989* (Washington: U.S. Government Printing Office, 1990).

The problem, however, is that since 1961 death rates for married persons have not been reported separately. Yet we know that married persons have somewhat lower death rates than unmarried persons. Davis estimated the number of deaths of married persons for 1965 and 1970; I have done so for 1989, using the following procedure. I compared the death rates for married persons by age and sex in 1960 with the death rates by age and sex for all persons in 1960. From this comparison I calculated the ratio of the death rate for married persons to the rate for all persons in each age-sex group. These ratios were typically in the range of 0.8 to 0.9. I then multiplied the death rates for all persons by age and sex in 1989 by the corresponding ratios, thereby adjusting the total death rates in 1989 to reflect the somewhat lower risk of death for married persons. This adjustment assumes that the ratio of the death rates of married persons to all persons has stayed the same for each age-sex group between 1960 and 1989, an assumption that seems reasonable for the purposes of this chapter. I then multiplied each adjusted death rate by the number of married people in the appropriate age-sex group (obtained from Current Population Reports, series P-20, no. 445), yielding an estimate of 975,666 deaths to married persons in 1989. The figures used in calculating the total rate of dissolution were as follows: (1) deaths of married persons in 1989: 975,666; (2) divorces in 1989: 1,163,000; (3) existing marriages in 1989:

55,284,000; (4) deaths per 1,000 existing marriages: 17.6; (5) divorces per 1,000 existing marriages: 21.0; and, finally, (6) total dissolutions per 1,000 existing marriages: 38.7.

41. For the first edition, I estimated that there were 906,300 deaths of married persons in 1978, as opposed to 1,128,000 divorces.

42. James A. Sweet and Larry L. Bumpass, *American Families and Households* (New York: Russell Sage Foundation, 1987).

43. Larry L. Bumpass, "Children and Marital Disruption: A Replication and Update," *Demography* 21 (November 1984): 71–82. Bumpass estimates experience of disruption by age sixteen as 22 percent at the rates of 1963–1965 and 43 percent at the rates of 1977–1979 (which were slightly higher than the rates prevalent at the end of the 1980s).

44. U.S. Bureau of the Census, Current Population Reports, series P-20, no. 450, "Marital Status and Living Arrangements: March 1990" (Washington: U.S. Government Printing Office, 1991).

45. U.S. Bureau of the Census, Current Population Reports, series P-20, no. 447, "Household and Family Characteristics: March 1990 and 1989" (Washington: U.S. Government Printing Office, 1991), Table 1; and U.S. Bureau of the Census, Current Population Reports, series P-20, no. 218, "Household and Family Characteristics: March 1970" (Washington: U.S. Government Printing Office, 1971), Table 1.

46. James A. Sweet, "The Living Arrangements of Separated, Widowed, and Divorced Mothers," *Demography* 9 (Feb. 1972): 143–157.

47. Bumpass, "Children and Marital Disruption."

48. The Bureau of the Census does provide annual information in its Current Population Survey on the number of people who were separated from their spouses at the time of the survey, but the figures are difficult to interpret for two reasons. First, the number of people currently separated depends not only on the rate at which people become separated but also on the rate at which they stop being separated—that is, on how quickly they divorce or reconcile once they have separated. As a result, the number of people currently separated could increase over time merely because separated spouses were taking more time to obtain their divorces, even if the overall rate of divorce were decreasing. Second, demographers suspect that the category "currently separated" is not accurately reported in surveys. The March 1989 Current Population Survey (U.S. Bureau of the Census, *Current Population Reports,* Series P-20, no. 445, "Marital Status and Living Arrangements: March 1989," U.S. Government Printing Office, 1990), for example, reported the following impossible situation: 2,671,000 women were separated from their husbands, but only 1,712,000 men were

separated from their wives. It seems likely that some of the so-called separated women had never married their supposed husbands and that some men who actually were separated from their wives reported instead that they had never married.

49. Sweet and Bumpass, *American Families and Households*.
50. John Demos, *A Little Commonwealth: Family Life in Plymouth Colony* (New York: Oxford University Press, 1970).
51. Paul H. Jacobson, *American Marriage and Divorce* (New York: Rinehart, 1959).
52. U.S. National Center for Health Statistics, *Monthly Vital Statistics Report* 38, no. 12, supplement, "Advance Report of Final Marriage Statistics, 1987" (Washington: U.S. Government Printing Office, 1990).
53. Ibid.; and Jacobson, *American Marriage and Divorce*.
54. In 1970 there were 180 remarriages per 1,000 divorced women aged 25 to 44; in 1980 the rate was 123; in 1987 it was 129. See National Center for Health Statistics, "Final Marriage Statistics, 1987"; and Larry Bumpass, James Sweet, and Teresa Castro Martin, "Changing Patterns of Remarriage," *Journal of Marriage and the Family* 52 (August 1990): 747–756.
55. Bumpass, Sweet, and Cherlin, "The Role of Cohabitation."
56. Bumpass and Sweet, "National Estimates."
57. Sweet and Bumpass, *American Families and Households*.
58. Ibid.
59. This figure is from unpublished NSFH data kindly provided by James Sweet and Elizabeth Thomson. The calculation excludes children born to cohabiting mothers and children living with one natural parent and a cohabiting partner.
60. Sweet and Bumpass, *American Families and Households*.

## 2. Explanations

1. Harold F. Dorn, "Pitfalls in Population Forecasts and Projections," *Journal of the American Statistical Association* 45 (Sept. 1950): 311–334.
2. I thank Susan Cotts Watkins for the "something in the air" phrase and for other helpful comments on this section.
3. Age explanations constitute a third general class: those that refer to the effects of the aging process. An older population, for example, will produce fewer babies each year than will a younger population. In the case of marriage and divorce since World War II, however, large changes have occurred in the experiences of comparable age groups; married men and women in their twenties in 1980 had a much higher probability of divorc-

ing than did married men and women in their twenties in 1960. Therefore, no age explanation can account for more than a small part of the changes in marriage and divorce in recent years.

4. See Arland Thornton and Willard L. Rodgers, "The Influence of Individual and Historical Time on Marital Dissolution," *Demography* 24 (February 1987): 1–22.

5. It is possible to construct a complex explanation of these parallel lines that is consistent with cohort effects. One might argue, for example, that in the 1950s the young women of the depression cohort, for reasons specific to their history, married early and had children quickly while older women were catching up for time lost during the war. But the period effects explanation is more parsimonious.

6. U.S. Bureau of the Census, Current Population Reports, series P-20, no. 349, "Marital Status and Living Arrangements: March 1979" (Washington: U.S. Government Printing Office, 1980), Table A.

7. U.S. Bureau of the Census, *Historical Statistics of the United States, Colonial Times to 1970*, bicentennial ed., pt. 1, series B-11 (Washington: U.S. Government Printing Office, 1975). The precise estimate was 3.8 children per woman.

8. See John R. Seeley, R. Alexander Sim, and Elizabeth W. Loosley, *Crestwood Heights* (New York: Basic Books, 1956); A. C. Spectorsky, *The Exurbanites* (New York: Lippincott, 1955); and William H. Whyte, Jr., *The Organization Man* (New York: Simon and Schuster, 1956).

9. Frank Levy, *Dollars and Dreams: The Changing American Income Distribution* (New York: Russell Sage Foundation, 1987).

10. Historian Elaine Tyler May makes this point in *Homeward Bound: American Families in the Cold War Era* (New York: Basic Books, 1988).

11. Ansley J. Coale and Susan Cotts Watkins, eds., *The Decline of Fertility in Europe* (Princeton: Princeton University Press, 1986).

12. This argument is advanced by Susan Cotts Watkins for Western Europe in "From Local to National Communities: The Transformation of Demographic Regimes in Western Europe, 1870–1960," *Population and Development Review* 16 (June 1990): 241–272.

13. See, for example, Betty Friedan, *The Feminine Mystique* (New York: W.W. Norton, 1963), chap. 8.

14. Randall Collins, *Sociology of Marriage and the Family: Gender, Love, and Property* (Chicago: Nelson-Hall, 1985).

15. The classic study is Elizabeth Bott, *Family and Social Network* (London: Tavistock Publications, 1957). See also Herbert Gans, *The Urban Villagers* (New York: The Free Press, 1962). On childrearing values, see Melvin L.

Kohn, *Class and Conformity: A Study in Values* (Homewood, Illinois: Dorsey Press, 1969).

16. See May, *Homeward Bound.* The common criticism in the media was that suburban families were too "permissive" in childrearing; see William H. Chafe, *The Unfinished Journey: America since World War II* (New York: Oxford University Press, 1986). But this criticism probably was overdrawn, as noted in Herbert Gans, *The Levittowners* (New York: Random House, 1967).

17. Brigitte Berger and Peter L. Berger describe the bourgeois family of the 1950s at length in *The War over the Family: Capturing the Middle Ground* (Garden City: Anchor Press, 1983). They emphasize such characteristics as its autonomous nature, its central concern for children, the importance of romantic love and intense affection between spouses, and its emphasis on women as the keepers of the home and moral guardians.

18. Ron Lesthaeghe and Johan Surkyn, "Cultural Dynamics and Economic Theories of Fertility Change," *Population and Development Review* 14 (March 1988): 1–45.

19. May, *Homeward Bound.*

20. The number of bachelor's or first professional degrees conferred by institutions of higher education rose from 81 per 1,000 persons 23 years old in 1940 to 182 per 1,000 in 1960. U.S. Bureau of the Census, *Historical Statistics of the United States: Colonial Times to 1970* (Washington: U.S. Government Printing Office, 1975), series H 755.

21. Norman B. Ryder, "Recent Trends and Group Differences in Fertility," in Charles F. Westoff, ed., *Toward the End of Growth* (Englewood Cliffs, N.J.: Prentice-Hall, 1973), pp. 57–68; and Judith Blake and Prithwis Das Gupta, "Reply," *Population and Development Review* 4 (June 1978): 326–329.

22. Lawrence Stone describes the emergence of "affective individualism" among the bourgeois and landed gentry in his book, *The Family, Sex, and Marriage in England 1500–1800* (New York: Harper and Row, 1977).

23. May writes of the persistent quest for intimacy in the postwar period in *Homeward Bound.* See also Louis Roussel, *La famille incertaine* (Paris: Editions Odile Jacob, 1989); and Ron Lesthaeghe, "A Century of Demographic and Cultural Change in Europe: An Exploration of Underlying Dimensions," *Population and Development Review* 9 (September 1983): 411–435.

24. Mirra Komarovsky, *The Unemployed Man and His Family* (New York: Dryden Press, 1940), p. 98.

25. Ibid., pp. 100–101.

26. Glen H. Elder, Jr., *Children of the Great Depression* (Chicago: University of Chicago Press, 1974).

27. Elder considered persons deprived if their families had suffered an income loss of more than 35 percent between 1929 and 1933. By this criterion, slightly more than half of the middle-class children and about two-thirds of the working-class children were classified as living in deprived homes.

28. Richard A. Easterlin, "What Will 1984 Be Like? Socioeconomic Implications of Recent Twists in the Age Structure," *Demography* 15 (Nov. 1978): 397–432; and Richard A. Easterlin, *Birth and Fortune: The Impact of Numbers on Personal Welfare* (New York: Basic Books, 1980).

29. Richard A. Easterlin, *Population, Labor Force, and Long Swings in Economic Growth* (New York: Columbia University Press, 1968), p. 124; and Komarovsky, *Unemployed Man.*

30. Charles F. Westoff, "Marriage and Fertility in the Developed Countries," *Scientific American* 239 (Dec. 1978): 51–57, at p. 53.

31. Although the data are not shown in Figure 2-3, the question was also asked in the 1975, 1976, 1977, and 1978 General Social Surveys. The results show that highest percentage favoring easier divorce occurred in 1974.

32. Arland Thornton, "Changing Attitudes toward Separation and Divorce: Causes and Consequences," *American Journal of Sociology* 90 (January 1985): 856–872.

33. Gerald C. Wright, Jr., and Dorothy N. Stetson, "The Impact of No-Fault Divorce Law Reform on Divorce in American States," *Journal of Marriage and the Family* 40 (Aug. 1978): 575–580. By 1985, all fifty states allowed some form of no-fault divorce. See Mary Ann Glendon, *The Transformation of Family Law: State, Law, and Family in the United States and Western Europe* (Chicago: University of Chicago Press, 1989).

34. Wright and Stetson, "The Impact of No-Fault Divorce Law Reform."

35. James A. Sweet and Larry L. Bumpass, *American Families and Households* (New York: Russell Sage Foundation, 1987).

36. Valerie Kincade Oppenheimer, *The Female Labor Force in the United States,* Population Monograph Series, no. 5 (Berkeley: Institute of International Studies, 1970); and U.S. Bureau of Labor Statistics, "Multi-Earner Families Increase," press release no. USDL 79–747, October 31, 1979.

37. U.S. Bureau of the Census, *Statistical Abstract of the United States, 1991* (Washington: U.S. Government Printing Office, 1991).

38. William P. Butz and Michael P. Ward, "The Emergence of Countercyclical U.S. Fertility," *American Economic Review* 69 (June 1979): 318–328; William P. Butz and Michael P. Ward, "Will U.S. Fertility Remain Low? A New

Economic Interpretation," *Population and Development Review* 5 (December 1979): 663–688; and Gary S. Becker, *A Treatise on the Family*, Enlarged Edition (Cambridge, Mass.: Harvard University Press, 1991).

39. Oppenheimer, *Female Labor Force.*

40. Easterlin, *Birth and Fortune.* For a discussion of explanations for the rise in female labor force participation, see Ralph E. Smith, "The Movement of Women into the Labor Force," in Ralph E. Smith, ed., *The Subtle Revolution: Women at Work* (Washington: Urban Institute, 1979), pp. 1–29.

41. Samuel H. Preston and Alan Thomas Richards, "The Influence of Women's Work Opportunities on Marriage Rates," *Demography* 12 (May 1975): 209–222; and Alan Freiden, "The United States Marriage Market," *Journal of Political Economy* 82, pt. 2 (March-April 1974): S34–S53.

42. Andrew Cherlin, "Postponing Marriage: The Influence of Young Women's Work Expectations," *Journal of Marriage and the Family* 42 (May 1980): 355–365.

43. Arthur W. Calhoun, *A Social History of the American Family*, vol. 3 (1919; reprint ed., New York: Barnes and Noble, 1960); Willard Waller, *The Family: A Dynamic Interpretation* (New York: Dryden, 1938); William J. Goode, *World Revolution and Family Patterns* (New York: Free Press, 1963); and Carl N. Degler, *At Odds: Women and the Family in America from the Revolution to the Present* (New York: Oxford University Press, 1980).

44. Early studies include Heather L. Ross and Isabel V. Sawhill, *Time of Transition: The Growth of Families Headed by Women* (Washington: Urban Institute, 1975); Andrew Cherlin, "Work Life and Marital Dissolution," in George Levinger and Oliver C. Moles, eds., *Divorce and Separation: Context, Causes, and Consequences* (New York: Basic Books, 1979), pp. 151–166; and Michael T. Hannan, Nancy Brandon Tuma, and Lyle P. Groeneveld, "Income and Independence Effects on Marital Dissolution: Results from the Seattle and Denver Income-Maintenance Experiments," *American Journal of Sociology* 84 (Nov. 1978): 611–633. Two recent analyses that also review the literature are Glenna Spitze and Scott J. South, "Women's Employment, Time Expenditure, and Divorce," *Journal of Family Issues* 6 (September 1985): 307–329; and Theodore N. Greenstein, "Marital Disruption and the Employment of Married Women," *Journal of Marriage and the Family* 52 (August 1990): 657–676.

45. For a discussion of these other characteristics, see Andrew Cherlin, "The Effect of Children on Marital Dissolution," *Demography* 14 (Aug. 1977): 265–272; and Larry L. Bumpass and James A. Sweet, "Differentials in Marital Instability: 1970," *American Sociological Review* 37 (Dec. 1972): 754–766.

46. William R. Johnson and Jonathan Skinner, "Labor Supply and Marital Separation," *American Economic Review* 76 (June 1986): 455–469.

47. Easterlin, *Birth and Fortune.*

48. Divorce rates also rose in parallel for women in their twenties and thirties. See Thornton and Rogers, "The Influence of Family and Historical Time."

49. In addition, research on the behavior of individuals over time offers little support for his thesis; one study of a group of high school seniors who were followed for several years found little evidence that their income position, relative to their parents' income, influenced their timing of marriage. See Maurice M. MacDonald and Ronald R. Rindfuss, "Earnings, Relative Income, and Family Formation," *Demography* 18 (May 1981): 123–136.

50. Charles F. Westoff and Norman B. Ryder, *The Contraceptive Revolution* (Princeton: Princeton University Press, 1977); and Charles F. Westoff and Elise F. Jones, "Patterns of Aggregate and Individual Changes in Contraceptive Practice, United States, 1965–1975," U.S. National Center for Health Statistics, Vital and Health Statistics, series 3, no. 17 (Washington: U.S. Government Printing Office, 1979).

51. Judith Blake and Prithwis Das Gupta, "Reproductive Motivation versus Contraceptive Technology: Is Recent American Experience an Exception?" *Population and Development Review* 1 (Dec. 1975): 229–249; and Norman B. Ryder, "On the Time Series of American Fertility," and Blake and Das Gupta, "Reply," both in *Population and Development Review* 4 (June 1978): 322–329.

52. See, for example, Easterlin, *Birth and Fortune,* pp. 55–57.

53. See James C. Cramer, "Fertility and Female Employment: Problems of Causal Direction," *American Sociological Review* 45 (April 1980): 167–190.

54. In addition, some demographers advanced the idea of a "marriage squeeze" to account for some of the postponement of marriage in the 1960s and 1970s. In our society, women tend to marry men who are a few years older than they are. The young men and women who came of age in the 1960s and 1970s were born at a time of rising birth rates. Consequently, after 1960 there were more twenty-year-old women, say, than there were men aged twenty-one or twenty-two. The result of this difference in numbers, some believe, was a "marriage squeeze"; unable to find suitable partners, some women postponed marrying. See, for example, Hugh Carter and Paul C. Glick, *Marriage and Divorce: A Social and Economic Study,* rev. ed. (Cambridge, Mass.: Harvard University Press, 1976). But by the end of the 1960s a serious flaw in the marriage model had become apparent. After 1980, the squeeze should have been reversed

as cohorts born during a time of falling birth rates were reaching adult-hood. Yet women's average age at marriage continued to climb throughout the decade.

55. Easterlin, *Birth and Fortune.*

56. These figures come from my tabulations of data from the General Social Surveys, 1972–1989, conducted by the National Opinion Research Center.

57. Frank Levy, *Dollars and Dreams: The Changing American Income Distribu-tion* (New York: Russell Sage Foundation, 1987).

58. Ibid.

59. See, for example, Barry Bluestone and Bennett Harrison, *The Deindustri-alization of America* (New York: Basic Books, 1982).

60. Levy, *Dollars and Dreams,* p. 100.

61. Levy made this point at a congressional staff briefing in January 1991, in which we both took part.

62. Michael B. Katz, *The People of Hamilton, Canada West: Family and Class in a Mid-Nineteenth-Century City* (Cambridge, Mass.: Harvard University Press, 1975), p. 292.

## 3. Consequences

1. On cohabitation and divorce, see Chapter 1. On proportion never-married at age 30, see James A. Sweet and Larry L. Bumpass, *American Families and Households* (New York: Russell Sage Foundation, 1987).

2. Robert Schoen, William Urton, Karen Woodrow, and John Baj used U.S. Bureau of the Census and U.S. Vital Statistics data in their article, "Mar-riage and Divorce in Twentieth Century American Cohorts," *Demography* 22 (February 1985): 101–114. For the 1908–1912, 1928–1932, and 1948–1950 cohorts of women, respectively, the following estimates were pro-duced: proportion ever-marrying of those surviving to age 15: .93, .97, and .95; proportion of marriages ending in divorce: .24, .32, and .42; proportion of divorced persons remarrying: .78, .73, and .77. The estimates for second divorces came from U.S. Bureau of the Census, Current Pop-ulation Reports, series P-20, no. 297, "Number, Timing, and Duration of Marriages and Divorces in the United States: June 1975" (Washington: U.S. Government Printing Office, 1976). Table G presents estimates of the "percent of persons married twice whose second marriage may eventually end in redivorce." The cohorts are grouped differently in this table than in the Schoen et al. table, so I interpolated. For the 1908–1912 cohort I used a second divorce probability of .11; for the 1928–1932 cohort I used .25, and for the 1948–1950 cohort I used .44.

3. Following the figures discussed in Chapter 1, I assumed that 88 percent of the women would eventually marry; 50 percent of those who married would divorce, and 67 percent of those who divorced would remarry. Good information on second divorces is scarce. As discussed in Chapter 1, the probability of divorce is somewhat higher in remarriages than in first marriages; I have used a figure of 55 percent. Paul C. Glick estimated that 54 percent of remarried women who were in their thirties in 1980 would eventually divorce. See his article, "Marriage, Divorce, and Living Arrangements: Prospective Changes," *Journal of Family Issues* 5 (March 1984): 7–26.

4. These percentages are products of the corresponding figures from notes 2 and 3. For example, the proportion ever-marrying and divorcing for the oldest cohort is (.93 × .24 × 100) = 22 percent. The Schoen et al. estimates of proportions divorcing are higher for earlier birth cohorts and lower for more recent cohorts than other demographic estimates. Thus they suggest that the increase in divorce in the twentieth century, although still dramatic, may not be as large as had been thought. Schoen and his collaborators used contemporaneous data on the earlier cohorts, whereas other demographers have used retrospective reports by members of the earlier cohorts who survived until the 1970s or 1980s. For example, Thomas J. Espenshade and Rachel Eisenberg Braun estimated on the basis of retrospective reports from the June 1975 Current Population Survey that 11.8 percent of the first marriages of women born between 1905 and 1909 would end in divorce; see their article "Life Course Analysis and Multistate Demography: An Application to Marriage, Divorce, and Remarriage," *Journal of Marriage and the Family* 44 (November 1982): 1025–36. Compare the Schoen et al. estimate of 22 percent for the 1908–1912 cohort of women. Schoen's data would seem to be more representative of earlier cohorts, but his estimates for recent cohorts, calculated in the same manner, are low by comparison with other vital statistics–based estimates. As I stated in Chapter 1, I do not think it is possible to resolve these differences in method and data at the present time. I have used Schoen's estimates as the basis for Figure 3-1 because he and his collaborators are the only group to apply a consistent method across all birth cohorts from the 1890s to the mid-century.

5. Schoen et al., "Marriage and Divorce," Table 2. The decline in average age at divorce was from 37.4 to 33.8. The decline in age at remarriage after divorce was from 38.2 to 35.9. For the youngest cohort, we know that age at marriage has been rising and that the median time to divorce has not changed much (see Sweet and Bumpass, *American Families and House-*

*holds*); so the age at divorce—and very likely the age at remarriage—should rise.

6. U.S. Bureau of the Census, Current Population Reports, Series P-20, No. 447, "Household and Family Characteristics: March 1990 and 1989" (Washington: U.S. Government Printing Office, 1991), Table 10; and U.S. Bureau of the Census, Current Population Reports, Series P-20, No. 218, "Household and Family Characteristics: March 1970" (Washington: U.S. Government Printing Office, 1971), Table 13. The 1990 figure is 4,751,000 separated or divorced female householders with their own children under 18, and the corresponding 1970 figure is 1,720,000.

7. U.S. Bureau of the Census, *Current Population Reports,* Series P-23, No. 162, "Studies in Marriage and the Family: Married Couple Families with Children" (Washington: U.S. Government Printing Office, 1989), Table B. The figure is 4,469,000.

8. Because the number of unmarried young adults has risen so rapidly as marriage ages have risen, the proportion of *all* young adults (including those who are married) who are living with their parents actually has risen since 1970. See Sweet and Bumpass, *American Families and Households.*

9. Ibid.

10. U.S. Bureau of the Census, "Household and Family Characteristics: March 1990 and 1989," Table B.

11. George Masnick and Mary Jo Bane, *The Nation's Families: 1960–1990* (Boston: Auburn House, 1980).

12. Mary Jo Bane, *Here to Stay: American Families in the Twentieth Century* (New York: Basic Books, 1976).

13. For now-classic statements on the "loss of functions" and the specialization of the family in emotional support and child socialization, see William F. Ogburn, "The Changing Family," *The Family* 19 (1938): 139–143; and Talcott Parsons and Robert F. Bales, *Family, Socialization, and Interaction Process* (New York: Free Press, 1955).

14. Judith Blake, "Structural Differentiation and the Family: A Quiet Revolution," in Amos H. Hawley, ed., *Societal Growth: Processes and Implications* (New York: Free Press, 1979), pp. 179–201.

15. See, for example, James L. Peterson and Nicholas Zill, "Marital Disruption, Parent-Child Relationships, and Behavior Problems in Children," *Journal of Marriage and the Family* 48 (May 1986): 295–307.

16. P. Lindsay Chase-Lansdale and E. Mavis Hetherington, "The Impact of Divorce on Life-Span Development: Short and Longterm Effects," in Paul B. Baltes, David L. Featherman, and Richard M. Lerner, eds., *Life-Span*

*Development and Behavior,* vol. 10 (Hillsdale, N.J.: Lawrence Erlbaum Associates, 1990), pp. 105–150.

17. E. Mavis Hetherington, Martha Cox, and Roger Cox, "The Aftermath of Divorce," in J. H. Stevens, Jr., and M. Matthews, eds., *Mother-Child, Father-Child Relations* (Washington: National Association for the Education of Young Children, 1978), pp. 146–176.

18. Robert S. Weiss, *Going It Alone: The Family Life and Social Situation of the Single Parent* (New York: Basic Books, 1979).

19. U.S. Bureau of the Census, Current Population Reports, series P-60, no. 173, "Child Support and Alimony: 1989" (Washington: U.S. Government Printing Office, 1991), Tables 1 and 3. The proportion of never-married women who receive any child support payments is even lower.

20. Saul D. Hoffman and Greg J. Duncan, "What *Are* the Economic Consequences of Divorce?" *Demography* 25 (November 1988): 641–645. Hoffman and Duncan demonstrate convincingly that Lenore J. Weitzman's widely cited estimate of the decline in women's standard of living after the breakup (73 percent, on average) is exaggerated and inconsistent with other figures in her book, *The Divorce Revolution: The Unexpected Social and Economic Consequences for Women and Children in America* (New York: Free Press, 1985). Her estimate of the rise in men's standard of living (42 percent) is almost certainly exaggerated also.

21. Greg J. Duncan and Saul D. Hoffman, "Economic Consequences of Marital Instability," in Martin David and Timothy Smeeding, eds., *Horizontal Equity, Uncertainty, and Economic Well-Being* (Chicago: University of Chicago Press, 1985), pp. 427–467. See Table 14.A.5.

22. Weiss, *Going It Alone.*

23. Janet A. Kohen, Carol A. Brown, and Roslyn Feldberg, "Divorced Mothers: The Costs and Benefits of Female Family Control," in George Levinger and Oliver C. Moles, eds., *Divorce and Separation: Context, Causes, and Consequences* (New York: Basic Books, 1979), pp. 228–245.

24. Robert S. Weiss, *Marital Separation* (New York: Basic Books, 1975).

25. Ibid.

26. Judith S. Wallerstein and Joan Berlin Kelly, *Surviving the Breakup: How Children and Parents Cope with Divorce* (New York: Basic Books, 1980).

27. Chase-Lansdale and Hetherington, "The Impact of Divorce." See also Peterson and Zill, "Marital Disruption."

28. G. R. Patterson, *Coercive Family Process* (Eugene, Oregon: Castalia Publishing Company, 1982).

29. Chase-Lansdale and Hetherington, "The Impact of Divorce."

30. Hetherington, Cox, and Cox, "Aftermath of Divorce."

31. E. Mavis Hetherington, "Family Relations Six Years after Divorce," in Kay Pasley and Marilyn Ihinger-Tallman, eds., *Remarriage and Stepparenting: Current Research and Theory* (New York: Guilford Press, 1987), pp. 185–205.

32. Judith S. Wallerstein and Sandra Blakeslee, *Second Chances: Men, Women, and Children a Decade after Divorce* (New York: Ticknor and Fields, 1989).

33. Families with children who had severe psychiatric problems were excluded, but parents often entered the study with a long history of psychiatric problems. As Wallerstein acknowledges in an earlier book, nearly 50 percent were "moderately disturbed or frequently incapacitated by disabling neuroses and addictions." Some were "chronically depressed" or "sometimes suicidal." Another 15 to 20 percent were characterized as "severely disturbed," with long histories of mental illness and chronic inability to cope with the demands of life (Wallerstein and Kelly, *Surviving the Breakup*, p. 328). Only a third of the sample were deemed to possess "adequate psychological functioning" prior to the divorce. We are never told what, if any, bearing parents' psychological histories had on their capacity to cope with divorce or to respond to the challenges of being a parent. Wallerstein and Blakeslee express great surprise at how many of the couples had difficulty adjusting to life after divorce, how many entered troubled second marriages, and how many had serious problems as parents. But given their psychological histories, the difficulties should have been anticipated. See Andrew Cherlin and Frank F. Furstenberg, Jr., "Divorce Doesn't Always Hurt the Kids," *The Washington Post*, March 19, 1989, p. C3.

34. Sara McLanahan, "Family Structure and the Reproduction of Poverty," *American Journal of Sociology* 90 (January 1985): 873–901; and Sara McLanahan and Larry L. Bumpass, "Intergenerational Consequences of Family Disruption," *American Journal of Sociology* 94 (July 1988): 130–152.

35. McLanahan summarizes her research findings in the newsletter of the Institute for Research on Poverty at the University of Wisconsin: Sara McLanahan, "The Consequences of Single Parenthood for Subsequent Generations," *Focus* 11 (Fall 1988): 16–21.

36. The .14 and .25 figures are estimates derived from the results in McLanahan and Bumpass, "Intergenerational Consequences," and are only illustrative. The authors also combine the experience of parental marital disruption with the experience of living with a never-married mother; further results suggest that the difference between these two groups is small.

37. E. Mavis Hetherington, "Coping with Family Transitions: Winners, Losers, and Survivors," *Child Development* 60 (1989): 1–14.
38. Hetherington, "Family Relations Six Years after Divorce," and "Coping with Family Transitions."
39. Peterson and Zill, "Marital Disruption."
40. Christy M. Buchanan, "Variation in Adjustment to Divorce: The Role of Feeling Caught in the Middle between Parents," paper presented at the biennial meeting of the Society for Research in Child Development, Seattle, April 18, 1991.
41. Chase-Lansdale and Hetherington, "Impact of Divorce."
42. For a review see Robert E. Emery, *Marriage, Divorce, and Children's Adjustment* (Beverly Hills: Sage Publications, 1988), pp. 85–86.
43. The payment of child support by noncustodial fathers, however, was associated with fewer behavioral problems. See Frank F. Furstenberg, Jr., S. Philip Morgan, and Paul D. Allison, "Paternal Participation and Children's Well-Being after Marital Dissolution," *American Sociological Review* 52 (October 1987): 695–701.
44. Frank F. Furstenberg, Jr., Christine Winquist Nord, James L. Peterson, and Nicholas Zill, "The Life Course of Children after Divorce, " *American Sociological Review* 48 (October 1983): 656–668.
45. John Demos, *A Little Commonwealth: Family Life in Plymouth Colony* (New York: Oxford University Press, 1970).
46. Wallerstein and Kelly, *Surviving the Breakup,* reported that the inclusion of the noncustodial father in the child's view of his family is common when the father continues to see the child.
47. Andrew Cherlin and James McCarthy, "Remarried Couple Households: Data from the June 1980 Current Population Survey," *Journal of Marriage and the Family* 47 (February 1985): 23–30.
48. Paul Bohannan, "Divorce Chains, Households of Remarriage, and Multiple Divorces," in Paul Bohannan, ed., *Divorce and After* (New York: Doubleday, 1970), pp. 127–139.
49. Frank F. Furstenberg, Jr., and Christine Winquist Nord, "Parenting Apart: Patterns of Childrearing after Marital Dissolution," *Journal of Marriage and the Family* 47 (November 1985): 893–904.
50. Eleanor E. Maccoby, Charlene E. Depner, and Robert H. Mnookin, "Coparenting in the Second and Fourth Years Following Parental Separation," unpublished manuscript, Stanford University, 1990. See also Eleanor E. Maccoby and Robert H. Mnookin, *Dividing the Child: Social and Legal Dilemmas of Custody* (Cambridge, Mass.: Harvard University Press, 1992).
51. See my article, "Remarriage as an Incomplete Institution," *American Jour-*

*nal of Sociology* 84 (Nov. 1978): 634–650, from which I draw heavily in this section.

52. See, for example, Nicholas Zill, "Behavior, Achievement, and Health Problems among Children in Stepfamilies: Findings from a National Survey of Child Health," in E. Mavis Hetherington and Joseph D. Arasteh, eds., *Impact of Divorce, Single Parenting, and Stepparenting on Children* (Hillsdale, N.J.: Lawrence Erlbaum Associates, 1988); pp. 325–368.

53. See the following reports on small-scale, intensive studies by psychologists: James H. Bray, "Children's Development during Early Remarriage," in Hetherington and Arasteh, *Impact of Divorce;* Hetherington, "Family Relations Six Years after Divorce;" Eulalee Brand, Glenn Clingempeel, and Kathryn Bowen-Woodward, "Family Relationships and Children's Psychological Adjustment in Stepmother and Stepfather Families," in Hetherington and Arasteh, *Impact of Divorce;* and J. W. Santrock, R. A. Warshak, C. Lindberg, and L. Meadows, "Children's and Parents' Observed Social Behavior in Stepfather Families," *Child Development* 53 (1982): 472–480. Two reports on the 1981 National Survey of Children provide at least partial confirmation that girls seem to react more negatively to the introduction of a stepparent than do boys: Paul Allison and Frank F. Furstenberg, Jr., "How Marital Dissolution Affects Children," *Developmental Psychology* 25 (1989): 540–549; and Peterson and Zill, "Marital Disruption." An analysis of the 1981 Child Health Supplement to the National Health Interview Survey, however, found only small differences between girls and boys: Zill, "Behavior, Achievement, and Health Problems."

54. Bray, "Children's Development during Early Remarriage."

55. See Chase-Lansdale and Hetherington, "The Impact of Divorce," for a review.

56. E. Mavis Hetherington and W. Glenn Clingempeel, *Coping with Marital Transitions: A Family Systems Perspective* (in press).

57. Furstenberg et al., "The Life Course of Children of Divorce."

58. Zill, "Behavior, Achievement, and Health Problems."

59. U.S. Bureau of the Census, Current Population Reports, Series P-23, No. 162, "Studies in Marriage and the Family: Married-Couple Families with Children" (Washington: U.S. Government Printing Office, 1989), Table A.

60. See, for example, Terence C. Halliday, "Remarriage: The More Complete Institution?" *American Journal of Sociology* 86 (Nov. 1980): 630–635.

61. Frank F. Furstenberg, Jr., and Graham B. Spanier, "The Risk of Dissolution in Remarriage: An Examination of Cherlin's Hypothesis of Incomplete Institutionalization," *Family Process* 33 (1984): 433–442. See also, by the

same authors, *Recycling the Family: Remarriage after Divorce* (Beverly Hills: Sage Publications, 1984).

62. See Cherlin, "Remarriage as an Incomplete Institution."

63. Some support for my position came from a national study of married persons who were interviewed in 1980 and reinterviewed in 1983. The probability of divorce during the interval was higher among remarried couples, and it increased with the complexity of the remarriage. For example, the probability was higher when both spouses had been remarried than when just one had been; and it was higher when stepchildren were present than when they were not. See Lynn K. White and Alan Booth, "The Quality and Stability of Remarriages: The Role of Stepchildren," *American Sociological Review* (October 1985): 689–698.

64. Hetherington, Cox, and Cox, "Aftermath of Divorce"; and William J. Goode, *Women in Divorce* (New York: Free Press, 1956).

65. Andrew J. Cherlin, Frank F. Furstenberg, Jr., P. Lindsay Chase-Lansdale, Kathleen E. Kiernan, Philip K. Robins. Donna Ruane Morrison, and Julien O. Teitler, "Longitudinal Studies of Effects of Divorce on Children in Great Britain and the United States," *Science* 252 (June 7, 1991): 1386–89.

66. Wallerstein and Kelly, *Surviving the Breakup.*

67. Cherlin et al., "Longitudinal Studies of Effects of Divorce."

68. Paul R. Amato and Bruce Kieth, "Parental Divorce and the Well-Being of Children: A Meta-Analysis," *Psychological Bulletin* 110 (1991): 26–46. Quoted at p. 40.

## 4. Race and Poverty

1. Two demographers, for instance, carefully studied the trends in childbearing between World War II and 1979, expecting to find that some groups in the population had not followed the overall cycle of boom and bust. To their surprise, they found that virtually every group they looked at showed the same pattern—fertility peaked in the late 1950s and declined thereafter. See Ronald R. Rindfuss and James A. Sweet, *Postwar Fertility Trends and Differentials in the United States* (New York: Academic Press, 1977); and James A. Sweet and Ronald R. Rindfuss, "Those Ubiquitous Fertility Trends: United States, 1945–1979," *Social Biology* 30 (1983): 127–139. Others have found that religious differences decreased in the past few decades: the childbearing and divorce rates of Catholics and non-Catholics have converged, for example. See Elise F. Jones and Charles F. Westoff, "The End of 'Catholic' Fertility," *Demography* 16 (May 1979): 209–217;

and Larry L. Bumpass, Teresa Castro Martin, and James A. Sweet, "Background and Early Marital Factors in Marital Disruption," *Journal of Family Issues*, forthcoming.

2. In this chapter, I will use the terms *African American* and *black* synonymously. As I write, the former term is becoming increasingly popular, but the latter term still is used more often.

3. On fertility trends by race, see Rindfuss and Sweet, *Postwar Fertility Trends*. On divorce, see Paul Jacobson, *American Marriage and Divorce* (New York: Rinehart, 1959); and James A. Sweet and Larry L. Bumpass, *American Families and Households* (New York: Russell Sage Foundation, 1987).

4. Frank Levy, *Dollars and Dreams: The Changing American Income Distribution* (New York: Russell Sage Foundation, 1987).

5. Greg J. Duncan, *Years of Poverty, Years of Plenty* (Ann Arbor: Institute for Social Research, University of Michigan, 1984).

6. The critical perspective is described in Lee Rainwater and William L. Yancey, *The Moynihan Report and the Politics of Controversy* (Cambridge, Mass.: MIT Press, 1967). On strengths, see Harriette Pipes McAdoo, ed., *Black Families*, 2nd ed. (Newbury Park, Calif.: Sage Publications, 1988).

7. Until the 1960s, most national statistics were tabulated only by "color" (white versus nonwhite), not by "race" (white versus black). But the vast majority—usually 90 percent or more—of people in the nonwhite category were black.

8. Neil G. Bennett, David E. Bloom, and Patricia H. Craig, "The Divergence of Black and White Marriage Patterns," *American Journal of Sociology* 95 (November 1989): 692–722.

9. Willard C. Rodgers and Arland Thornton, "Changing Patterns of First Marriage in the United States," *Demography* 22 (1985): 265–279. Rodgers and Thornton base their estimates on the age-specific marriage rates for the 1977 to 1979 period.

10. Sweet and Bumpass, *American Families*.

11. Thomas Espenshade, "The Recent Decline of American Marriage: Blacks and Whites in Comparative Perspective," pp. 53–90 in Kingsley Davis and Amyra Grossbard-Schechtman, *Contemporary Marriage* (New York: Russell Sage Foundation, 1986).

12. Part of the decline is due to the increasing gap in life expectancy between women and men and the corresponding increase in the amount of time older women spend as widows. This trend, however, has affected blacks and whites similarly.

13. M. D. R. Evans, "American Fertility Patterns: A Comparison of White and

Nonwhite Cohorts Born in 1903–56," *Population and Development Review* 12 (June 1986): 267–293.

14. The racial differences in the trend toward postponing first births are demonstrated in Ronald R. Rindfuss, S. Philip Morgan, and Gray Swicegood, *First Births in America: Changes in the Timing of Parenthood* (Berkeley: University of California Press, 1988). Estimates of the proportion having any children can be found in Evans, "American Fertility Patterns."

15. Evans, "American Fertility Patterns."

16. U.S. National Center for Health Statistics, *Monthly Vital Statistics Report,* vol. 39, No. 4, Supplement, "Advance Report of Final Natality Statistics, 1988" (Washington: U.S. Government Printing Office, 1990).

17. National Center for Health Statistics, "Advance Report of Final Natality Statistics, 1988"; and Herbert L. Smith and Phillips Cutright, "Thinking about Change in Illegitimacy Ratios: United States, 1963–1983," *Demography* 25 (May 1988): 235–247.

18. Smith and Cutright, "Thinking about Change."

19. U.S. Bureau of the Census, *Current Population Reports,* Series P-20, No. 445, "Marital Status and Living Arrangements: March 1989" (Washington: U.S. Government Printing Office, 1990).

20. National Center for Health Statistics, "Advance Report of Final Natality Statistics, 1988."

21. Smith and Cutright, "Thinking about Change."

22. Bureau of the Census, "Marital Status and Living Arrangements, March 1989"; and National Center for Health Statistics, "Advance Report of Final Natality Statistics, 1988."

23. Bureau of the Census, "Marital Status and Living Arrangements: March 1989." These comparisons are discussed in more detail in Andrew J. Cherlin, "The Weakening Link between Marriage and the Care of Children," *Family Planning Perspectives* 20 (November-December 1988): 302–306.

24. Gary S. Becker, *A Treatise on the Family,* Enlarged Edition (Cambridge, Mass.: Harvard University Press, 1991).

25. See Talcott Parsons, "The Kinship System of the Contemporary United States," *American Anthropologist* 45 (1943): 22–38.

26. All statistics in this paragraph are from Reynolds Farley and Walter R. Allen, *The Color Line and the Quality of Life in America* (New York: Russell Sage Foundation, 1987).

27. Reynolds Farley and Suzanne M. Bianchi, "The Growing Racial Difference in Marriage and Family Patterns," paper presented at the meetings of the

American Statistical Association, Chicago, August 1986. The figures that the authors compiled came from Current Population Survey data collected by the Bureau of the Census.

28. Reynolds Farley makes this point in "After the Starting Line: Blacks and Women in an Uphill Race," *Demography* 25 (November 1988): 477–495.

29. Murray, *Losing Ground*, and Becker, *A Treatise on the Family*.

30. David T. Ellwood and Lawrence H. Summers, "Poverty in America: Is Welfare the Answer or the Problem?" pp. 78–105 in Sheldon H. Danziger and Daniel H. Weinberg, eds., *Fighting Poverty: What Works and What Doesn't* (Cambridge, Mass.: Harvard University Press, 1986).

31. For example, Robert Moffitt recently analyzed Current Population Survey data for the period 1969 to 1985 and reported that the effects of welfare benefits on marital status were in the expected direction but generally weak. Nevertheless, the effects grew stronger during the period. See Moffitt, "The Effect of the U.S. Welfare System on Marital Status," *Journal of Public Economics*, forthcoming.

32. I calculated these percentages from unpublished tabulations from the March 1988 Current Population Survey provided to me kindly by the U.S. Bureau of Labor Statistics.

33. Pamela J. Smock, "Remarriage Patterns of Black and White Women: Reassessing the Role of Educational Attainment," *Demography* 27 (August 1990): 467–473.

34. See Robert Schoen and John Wooldredge, "Marriage Choices in North Carolina and Virginia, 1969–71 and 1979–81," *Journal of Marriage and the Family* 51 (May 1989): 465–481; James A. Sweet and Larry L. Bumpass, *American Families and Households* (New York: Russell Sage Foundation, 1987); and Graham B. Spanier and Paul C. Glick, "Mate Selection Differentials between Whites and Blacks in the United States," *Social Forces* 58 (March 1980): 707–725.

35. See Bennett et al., *The Divergence of Black and White Marriage Patterns*, Table 2, for Coale-McNeil estimates of lifetime probabilities of marriage for white and black women with varying levels of education.

36. Suzanne M. Bianchi and Daphne Spain, *American Women in Transition* (New York: Russell Sage Foundation, 1986).

37. M. Belinda Tucker and Claudia Mitchell-Kernan, "The Decline of Marriage among African Americans: Attitudinal Dimensions," paper presented at the Annual Convention of the American Psychological Association, New Orleans, August 1989.

38. M. Belinda Tucker and Claudia Mitchell-Kernan, "Sex Ratio Imbalance among Afro-Americans: Conceptual and Methodological Issues," in R.

Jones, ed., *Advances in Black Psychology, Volume 1* (Berkeley: Cobb and Henry, forthcoming).

39. These figures were obtained from Farley and Allen, *The Color Line,* p. 170. They incorporate corrections to the 1980 Census for the net undercount of black men.

40. I have made these calculations based on 1988 age-specific rates of firearm homicides, unintentional firearm deaths, and non-firearm suicides for black males. U.S. National Center for Health Statistics, *Monthly Vital Statistics Report,* vol. 39, No. 11, Supplement, "Firearm Mortality among Children, Youth and Young Adults 1–34 Years of Age, Trends and Current Status: United States, 1979–88" (Washington: U.S. Government Printing Office, 1991).

41. For historical statistics on black and white sex ratios, see M. Belinda Tucker and Claudia Mitchell-Kernan, "Sex Ratio Imbalance among Afro-Americans: Conceptual and Methodological Issues," in Jones, *Advances In Black Psychology* (forthcoming).

42. Sociologists have long theorized that there is more outmarriage among black men than among black women because black men can trade income for the culturally dominant physical characteristics or higher "caste" status of white women. But the evidence in support of this hypothesis is weak. See M. Belinda Tucker and Claudia Mitchell-Kernan, "New Trends in Black American Interracial Marriage," *Journal of Marriage and the Family* 52 (February 1990): 209–218, especially note 3.

43. Sweet and Bumpass, *American Families,* Table 2-10. See also Tucker and Mitchell-Kernan, "New Trends."

44. The most useful discussion of these factors is in William A. Darity, Jr., and Samuel L. Myers, Jr., "Family Structure and the Marginalization of Black Men," Afro-American Studies Program, University of Maryland, September 1989.

45. Patrick A. Langan, "The Prevalence of Imprisonment," *U.S. Bureau of Justice Statistics Special Report* (Washington: U.S. Government Printing Office, 1985). The report calculates that in 1979, 2.55 percent of black men aged 20 to 29 were in prison on any given day. Since the prison population has risen sharply since 1979, this estimate is probably conservative.

46. It is difficult to calculate a precise figure. Published data show breakdowns of admission rates by race and sex, and separately by race and age, but not by all three characteristics simultaneously. Alvin F. Poussaint cites unpublished data supplied by the National Institute of Mental Health to the President's Commission on Mental Health in 1978. According to these data, the admissions rate in 1975 was 892 per 100,000 black males age 18

to 24, and 1,033 per 100,000 black males age 25 to 44. The figures in the most recent published tables suggest that these rates have gone up since 1975. However, discharge rates also may have risen; and some individuals may be admitted more than once in a given year. See Poussaint, "The Mental Health Status of Blacks—1983," pp. 187–239 in National Urban League, *The State of Black America 1983* (Washington: National Urban League, Inc., 1983), Table 20; and U.S. Alcohol, Drug Abuse, and Mental Health Administration, *Mental Health, United States, 1987* (Washington: U.S. Government Printing Office, 1987), Tables 3.1 to 3.5.

47. Greg J. Duncan and Saul D. Hoffman, "Teenage Underclass Behavior and Subsequent Poverty: Have the Rules Changed?" pp. 155–174 in Christopher Jencks and Paul E. Peterson, eds., *The Urban Underclass* (Washington: Brookings Institution, 1991).

48. William Julius Wilson and Kathryn M. Neckerman, "Poverty and Family Structure: The Widening Gap between Evidence and Public Policy Issues," in Sheldon H. Danziger and Daniel H. Weinberg, *Fighting Poverty: What Works and What Doesn't* (Cambridge, Mass.: Harvard University Press, 1986), pp. 232–259.

49. Daniel T. Lichter, Felicia B. LeClere, and Diane K. McLaughlin, "Local Marriage Markets and the Marital Behavior of Black and White Women," *American Journal of Sociology* 96 (January 1991): 843–867.

50. William Julius Wilson, *The Truly Disadvantaged: The Inner City, the Underclass, and Public Policy* (Chicago: University of Chicago Press, 1987).

51. Few studies show convincingly that the movement of jobs to the suburbs is a significant factor in the worsening employment situation of black men. See Christopher Jencks and Susan Mayer, "Residential Segregation, Job Proximity, and Black Job Opportunities," Center for Urban Affairs and Policy Research, Northwestern University.

52. Duncan and Hoffman, "Teenage Underclass Behavior."

53. Levy, *Dollars and Dreams.*

54. Robert D. Mare and Christopher Winship, "Socioeconomic Change and the Decline of Marriage for Blacks and Whites," pp. 175–202 in Jencks and Peterson, *The Urban Underclass.*

55. David T. Ellwood and David T. Rodda, "The Hazards of Work and Marriage: The Influence of Male Employment on Marriage Rates," unpublished manuscript, Harvard University, 1990.

56. Saul D. Hoffman, Greg J. Duncan, and Ronald Mincy, "Marriage and Welfare Use among Young Women: Do Labor Market, Welfare and Neighborhood Factors Account for Declining Rates of Marriage among Black and White Women?" Paper presented at the annual meeting of the Population Association of America, Washington, D.C., March 1991.

57. Robert I. Lerman, "Employment Opportunities of Young Men and Family Formation," *Papers and Proceedings of the American Economic Association* 79 (May 1989): 62–66.

58. Lerman notes in "Employment Opportunities" that the Becker model implies that nearly all steadily employed black men should be married.

59. Christopher Jencks, "What Is the Underclass—and Is It Growing?" *Focus* 12 (Spring-Summer 1989): 14–26.

60. Mark Testa, Nan Marie Astone, Marilyn Krogh, and Kathryn M. Neckerman, "Employment and Marriage among Inner-City Fathers," *Annals of the American Academy of Political and Social Science* 501 (January 1989): 79–91.

61. Sweet and Bumpass, *American Families*, Table 3.21.

62. Ibid., Table 2.8.

63. Reynolds Farley and Walter R. Allen, *The Color Line and the Quality of Life in America* (New York: Russell Sage Foundation, 1987), Table 6.1 and associated discussion.

64. Andrew J. Cherlin and Frank F. Furstenberg, Jr., *The New American Grandparent: A Place in the Family, a Life Apart* (New York: Basic Books, 1986).

65. Harriette P. McAdoo, "Factors Related to Stability in Upwardly Mobile Black Families," *Journal of Marriage and the Family* 40 (1978): 761–776.

66. Susan Greenhalgh, "Fertility as Mobility: Sinic Transitions," *Population and Development Review* 14 (December 1988): 629–673, quoted at p. 668. I thank Nan Astone for discussions on this point.

67. Rubye Beck and Scott H. Beck, "The Incidence of Extended Households among Middle-Aged Black and White Women," *Journal of Family Issues* 10 (June 1989): 147–168.

68. Jacqueline Jones, *Labor of Love, Labor of Sorrow: Black Women and the Family from Slavery to the Present* (New York: Basic Books, 1985), quoted at p. 101.

69. Shepard Krech III, "Black Family Organization in the Nineteenth Century: An Ethnological Perspective," *Journal of Interdisciplinary History* 12 (Winter 1982): 429–452.

70. S. Philip Morgan, Antonio McDaniel, Andrew T. Miller, and Samuel H. Preston, "Racial Differences in Household and Family Structure at the Turn of the Century," paper presented at the Albany Conference on Demographic Perspectives on the American Family: Patterns and Prospects, State University of New York at Albany, April 6–7, 1990.

71. Herbert G. Gutman, *The Black Family in Slavery and Freedom, 1750–1925* (New York: Pantheon, 1976). For a review of this and similar studies, see Stanley L. Engerman, "Black Fertility and Family Structure in the U.S., 1880–1940," *Journal of Family History* 2 (Summer 1977): 117–138.

72. The classic work, first published in 1941 and recently reissued with an introduction to the debate by Sidney W. Mintz, is Melville J. Herskovits, *The Myth of the Negro Past* (Boston: Beacon Press, 1990).

73. Caroline Bledsoe, "Transformations in Sub-Saharan African Marriage and Fertility," *Annals of the American Academy of Political and Social Science* 501 (July 1990): 115–125.

74. Niara Sudarkasa, "African and Afro-American Family Structure: A Comparison," *The Black Scholar* (November-December 1980): 37–60; and "Interpreting the African Heritage in Afro-American Family Organization," pp. 37–53 in Harriette Pipes McAdoo, ed., *Black Families* (Beverly Hills: Sage Publications, 1981).

75. Jones, *Labor of Love*, p. 39.

76. In the 1981 edition of this book I wrote: "the causes of the recent divergence lie in the contemporary situation of urban, Northern blacks rather than in a lingering heritage of slavery or a clash of traditional and modern cultures. The family patterns of urban blacks differ today from the patterns among whites in large part because of differences in the current experiences of city-born-and-bred blacks and whites. Instead of looking back to slavery or to the rural, postbellum South, we need to look at life in the cities today." I now think that was an overstatement that paid too little attention to the historical roots of the recent changes.

77. James P. Smith, "Poverty and the Family," pp. 141–172 in Gary D. Sandefur and Marta Tienda, eds., *Divided Opportunities: Minorities, Poverty, and Social Policy* (New York: Plenum, 1988).

78. See, for example, Mary Jo Bane, "Household Composition and Poverty," pp. 209–231 in Sheldon H. Danziger and Daniel H. Weinberg, eds., *Fighting Poverty: What Works and What Doesn't* (Cambridge, Mass.: Harvard University Press, 1986).

79. Ibid.

80. Sara McLanahan, "Family Structure and the Reproduction of Poverty," *American Journal of Sociology* 90 (January 1985): 873–901; and Sara McLanahan and Larry L. Bumpass, "Intergenerational Consequences of Family Disruption," *American Journal of Sociology* 94 (July 1988): 130–152. McLanahan summarizes her research findings in "The Consequences of Single Parenthood for Subsequent Generations," *Focus* 11 (Fall 1988): 16–21.

81. Carol B. Stack, *All Our Kin* (New York: Harper and Row, 1974).

82. See, for example, Walter R. Allen, "The Search for Applicable Theories of Black Family Life," *Journal of Marriage and the Family* 40 (February 1978): 117–129.

83. Demitri Shimkin, Gloria Jean Louie, and Dennis A. Frate, "The Black Extended Family: A Basic Rural Institution and a Mechanism of Urban Adaptation," pp. 25–147 in Demitri B. Shimkin, Edith M. Shimkin, and Dennis A. Frate, *The Extended Family in Black Societies* (The Hague: Mouton, 1978).

84. Tamara K. Hareven, *Family Time and Industrial Time* (Cambridge: Cambridge University Press, 1982).

85. Stack, *All Our Kin.*

86. Frank F. Furstenberg, Jr., with Alisa Belzer, Colleen Davis, Judith A. Levine, Kristine Morrow, and Mary Washington, "How Families Manage Risk and Opportunity in Dangerous Neighborhoods," paper presented at the Annual Meetings of the American Sociological Association, Washington, D.C., August 1990.

87. Center for Labor Market Studies, Northeastern University, *Social and Economic Indicators for Families with Children* (Boston, 1990).

88. Katherine S. Newman makes this point in "Culture and Structure in *The Truly Disadvantaged:* An Anthropological Perspective." Paper presented at the Conference on *The Truly Disadvantaged,* October 1989.

89. According to the 1980 Census, 449,000 blacks lived in the city of Washington, and 405,000 lived in the remainder of the Washington metropolitan area (defined by the Census as the Washington Standard Metropolitan Statistical Area). U.S. Bureau of the Census, Census of Population, 1980, General Population Characteristics, Part 1, U.S. Summary, Chapter B (Washington: U.S. Government Printing Office, 1983), Table 69. The 1990 Census data, not available at this writing, probably will show that more blacks live in the Washington suburbs than in the city.

90. Dennis P. Hogan, Lingxin Hao, and William L. Parish, "Race, Kin Networks, and Assistance to Mother-Headed Families," *Social Forces* 68 (1990): 797–812.

91. William L. Parish, Lingxin Hao, and Dennis P. Hogan, "Family Networks, Welfare, and Work of Young Mothers," *Journal of Marriage and the Family* 53 (February 1991): 203–215.

92. See also Sheppard G. Kellam, Margaret A. Ensminger, and J. T. Turner, "Family Structure and the Mental Health of Children," *Archives of General Psychiatry* 34 (1977): 1012–22.

93. Linda M. Burton and Vern L. Bengtson, "Black Grandmothers: Issues of Timing and Continuity of Roles," pp. 61–77 in Vern L. Bengtson and Joan F. Robertson, eds., *Grandparenthood* (Beverly Hills: Sage Publications, 1985), p. 193.

94. Harriette Pipes McAdoo, "Transgenerational Patterns of Upward Mobility

in African American Families," pp. 148–168 in McAdoo, *Black Families*, quoted at p. 149.

95. National Commission on Children, *Beyond Rhetoric: A New American Agenda for Children and Families* (Washington: U.S. Government Printing Office, 1991).

96. Michael S. Teitlebaum and Jay M. Winter, *The Fear of Population Decline* (Orlando, Fla.: Academic Press, 1985).

97. Bennett et al., "The Divergence of Black and White Marriage Patterns."

98. See David T. Ellwood, *Poor Support: Poverty and the American Family* (New York: Basic Books, 1988).

99. E. Franklin Frazier, *The Negro Family in the United States* (Chicago: University of Chicago Press, 1939).

100. Cherlin and Furstenberg, "The New American Grandparent," p. 128.


## 5. The State of Our Unions

1. This section of the chapter is drawn from my account of the debate: Andrew Cherlin,"The Strange Career of the 'Harvard-Yale Study,'" *Public Opinion Quarterly* 54 (Spring 1990): 117–124.

2. On Sweden, see David Popenoe, *Disturbing the Nest: Family Change and Decline in Modern Societies* (New York: Aldine de Gruyter, 1988); and Britta Hoem and Jan M. Hoem, "The Swedish Family: Aspects of Contemporary Developments," *Journal of Family Issues* 9 (September 1988): 397–424.

3. Joseph Veroff, Elizabeth Douvan, and Richard A. Kulka, *The Inner American: A Self-Portrait from 1957 to 1976* (New York: Basic Books, 1981), quoted at p. 191.

4. Arland Thornton, "Changing Attitudes towards Family Issues in the United States," *Journal of Marriage and the Family* 51 (November 1989): 873–893.

5. See Robert N. Bellah, Richard Madsen, William M. Sullivan, Ann Swidler, and Steven M. Tipton, *Habits of the Heart: Individualism and Commitment in American Life* (Berkeley: University of California Press, 1985), especially Chapter 4, "Love and Marriage."

6. John Modell and Tamara K. Hareven, "Urbanization and the Malleable Household: An Examination of Boarding and Lodging in American Families," *Journal of Marriage and the Family* (August 1973): 467–479.

7. Frank Levy, *Dollars and Dreams: The Changing American Income Distribution* (New York: Russell Sage Foundation, 1987).

8. U.S. Bureau of the Census, *Historical Statistics of the United States, Colonial Times to 1970* (Washington: U.S. Government Printing Office).

9. Levy, *Dollars and Dreams*.
10. This story of rising incomes also doesn't work as well for the poor. In Chapter 4 it was noted that some theorists of the underclass argue that the deteriorating employment prospects of black men have reduced the economic value of marriage to black women. There are fewer lasting marriages, so this line of reasoning goes, not because economic partnerships are less necessary but because they are less possible.
11. Larry L. Bumpass, James A. Sweet, and Andrew Cherlin, "The Role of Cohabitation in Declining Rates of Marriage," *Journal of Marriage and the Family*, in press.
12. Arland Thornton and Deborah Freedman, "Changing Attitudes toward Marriage and Single Life," *Family Planning Perspectives* 14 (November-December 1982): 297–303.
13. Thornton, "Changing Attitudes toward Family Issues."
14. Ibid.
15. Bellah et al., *Habits of the Heart*, p. 109.
16. James A. Sweet and Larry L. Bumpass, *American Families and Households* (New York: Russell Sage Foundation, 1987).
17. Frank F. Furstenberg, Jr., J. Brooks-Gunn, and S. Philip Morgan, *Adolescent Mothers in Later Life* (Cambridge: Cambridge University Press, 1987).
18. Sara McLanahan and Larry L. Bumpass, "Intergenerational Consequences of Marital Disruption," *American Journal of Sociology* 94 (July 1988): 130–152.
19. See, for example, "Poverty amid Plenty," *The Wall Street Journal*, September 1, 1988, p. 20.
20. Mary Jo Bane, "Household Composition and Poverty," pp. 209–231 in Sheldon H. Danziger and Daniel H. Weinberg, eds., *Fighting Poverty: What Works and What Doesn't* (Cambridge, Mass.: Harvard University Press, 1986).
21. Greg J. Duncan and Saul D. Hoffman, "Economic Consequences of Marital Instability," pp. 427–467 in Martin David and Timothy Smeeding, eds., *Horizontal Equity, Uncertainty, and Economic Well-Being* (Chicago: University of Chicago Press, 1985).
22. Duncan and Hoffman, "Economic Consequences."
23. These programs figured prominently, for example, in the final report of the National Commission on Children, "Beyond Rhetoric: A New Agenda for Children and Families" (Washington: U.S. Government Printing Office, 1991).
24. Charles Murray, *Losing Ground: American Social Policy, 1950–1980* (New York: Basic Books, 1984).

25. Irwin S. Garfinkel and Sara S. McLanahan, *Single Mothers and Their Children: A New American Dilemma* (Washington, D.C.: The Urban Institute Press, 1986).

26. Garfinkel and McLanahan, *Single Mothers;* and David T. Ellwood, *Poor Support: Poverty in the American Family* (New York: Basic Books, 1988).

27. William Julius Wilson and Katherine M. Neckerman, "Poverty and Family Structure: The Widening Gap between Evidence and Public Policy Issues," pp. 232–259 in Danziger and Weinberg, *Fighting Poverty;* and William Julius Wilson, *The Truly Disadvantaged: The Inner City, The Underclass, and Public Policy* (Chicago: University of Chicago Press, 1987).

28. Thomas J. Espenshade, "The Recent Decline of American Marriage: Blacks and Whites in Comparative Perspective," in Kingsley Davis and Amyra Grossbard-Shechtman, eds., *Contemporary Marriage: Comparative Perspectives on a Changing Institution* (New York: Russell Sage Foundation, 1985), pp. 53–90.

29. Sweet and Bumpass, *American Families and Households.*

30. Ibid.

31. Walter R. Allen, "The Search for Applicable Theories of Black Family Life," *Journal of Marriage and the Family* 40 (February 1978): 117–129.

32. Randall Collins, *Sociology of Marriage and the Family: Gender, Love, and Property* (Chicago: Nelson-Hall, 1985); and Kingsley Davis, "The Meaning and Significance of Marriage in Contemporary Society," in Davis and Shechtman, *Contemporary Marriage.* All references in this section are to these two sources unless otherwise noted.

33. All of the statistics in this paragraph were cited earlier in the book with the exception of the number of teenage births, which is from James Trussell, "Teenage Pregnancy in the United States," *Family Planning Perspectives* 20 (November-December 1988): 262–272.

34. See Michael S. Teitelbaum and Jay M. Winter, *The Fear of Population Decline* (Orlando: Academic Press, 1985).

35. The loudest work so far is Ben J. Wattenberg, *The Birth Dearth: What Happens When People in Free Countries Don't Have Enough Babies?* (New York: Pharos Books, 1987).

36. The estimates are from special tabulations prepared by the World Bank and published in Wattenberg, *The Birth Dearth.*

37. Kingsley Davis, "Reproductive Institutions and the Pressure for Population," *Sociological Review* 29 (1937): 289–306, quoted at pp. 305–306. The quotation was reported in John Modell, "Historical Reflections on American Marriage," in David and Grossbard-Shechtman, *Contemporary Marriage,* pp. 181–196.

# Index

Abortion, 54, 55
Adolescents, 64–65; in the depression, 39–40, 42–43; response to divorce, 75, 76, 77–78
Africa, 110–112
African Americans. *See* Blacks
Age: at childbearing, 18, 96; at divorce, 68; at remarriage, 68. *See also* Age at marriage
Age at marriage, 2, 7, 8–10, 17, 29, 30, 55, 63; in 1970s and 1980s, 10, 45, 57; of blacks and whites, 91, 92–94, 95
Aid to Families with Dependent Children (AFDC), 100, 122, 134–135
Allen, Walter R., 107
Allison, Paul, 77–78
Amato, Paul R., 89
Attitudes: toward families, 35–38, 40–41, 43, 126–127; toward working women, 36, 57–61, 63; toward divorce, 45–49, 56, 126; toward childlessness, 126; toward marriage, 126–130, 132–133, 136–140; toward extramarital sex, 129

Baby boom, postwar, 6, 25, 29–30, 31, 34, 35, 139; and children of baby boomers, 6–7, 12–13, 20
Bane, Mary Jo, 114
Becker, Gary, 99, 100
Bennett, Neil G., 94, 124, 125
Birth control. *See* Contraception
Birth probabilities, 32–34
Birth rate, 2, 7, 18–20, 41, 98, 138; after World War II, 6, 18, 34–35, 38; Great Depression and, 6, 31, 41, 55; in 1980s and 1990s, 18, 19, 57, 138–139; in 1960s and 1970s, 18, 35, 44, 57
Blacks: marital separation among, 27, 95; remarriage among, 28, 95; and out-of-wedlock childbearing, 91, 96–98, 106–107, 111, 113, 136; poverty and, 91–92, 114–119, 136; and kin networks, 92, 107–112, 113, 115–122, 135;

cohabitation among, 95; education level of, 101–106 *passim;* employment among, 101–106, 112–113, 121, 135; mortality rates among, 102–103; incarceration and institutionalization rates among, 103; and intermarriage, 103, 107; earning power of, 103–104, 112–113, 121; and grandmothers, 107–108, 123, 118–119, 123; cultural and historical traditions of, 108–113, 120. *See also* Racial differences
Blake, Judith, 55, 71
Blakeslee, Sandra, 76
Bloom, David E., 94, 124, 125
Bohannan, Paul, 83
Breadwinner-homemaker family, 36–37, 99
Bumpass, Larry, 24, 77
Bureau of the Census, 27, 34, 67, 73, 98–99, 104, 105, 125
Burton, Linda, 119

Calhoun, Arthur W., 52
Chase-Lansdale, P. Lindsay, 72
Childbearing, 4, 7, 18–20, 60; cohabitation and, 15, 16, 17; out-of-wedlock, 15, 16, 17, 91, 96–98, 106–107, 111, 113; trends in, 18–20, 60–61, 95–98, 106–107; delayed or postponed, 19, 20, 57, 96
Child care, 118, 140
Childrearing, 130–131. *See also* Families
Children, 26, 37–38, 44–45, 130–131, 134; response to divorce, 26, 72–73, 75–80, 85, 87–89, 131–132; during the depression, 39–40, 42–43; working mothers and, 49, 58–59; in stepfamilies, 28, 80–86, 87, 89. *See also* Adolescents
Child support, 73, 122, 133–134, 140
Coercive cycles, 75, 76, 85
Cohabitation, 7, 8–9, 11–18, 70, 71, 125; before remarriage, 13, 28, 70, 80; duration of, 14, 16, 70, 129; among blacks, 95
Cohort analysis, 8